THE Seltzer METHOD
Drawing Dogs

TUTORIALS & SKETCHBOOK

© 2020 Jerry Joe Seltzer
All Rights Reserved

Written and illustrated by Jerry Joe Seltzer

For more information visit The SeltzerMethod.com

TABLE OF CONTENTS

Drawing a dog's head from the front... pgs 2-3
Drawing a dog's head from the side.... pgs 4-5
Drawing a dog's body from the side.... pgs 6-7
Drawing in 3 dimensions...................... pgs 8-11

Dog Breeds
Bernese Mountain Dog........................ pgs 12-19
Bichon Frise.. pgs 20-27
Bloodhound.. pgs 28-35
Chihuahua.. pgs 36-43
Collie... pgs 44-51
Dachshund... pgs 52-59
French Bulldog...................................... pgs 60-67
German Shepherd................................ pgs 68-75
Great Dane.. pgs 76-83
Golden Retriever.................................. pgs 84-91
Greyhound... pgs 92-99
Poodle... pgs 100-107
Saint Bernard.. pgs 108-115
Wolf... pgs 116-123

Extra sketching pages.......................... pgs 124+

Drawing a dog's head from the front

Starting With A Circle

The first step to drawing a dog's head, or really any head, is making a circle. Some artists find it hard to draw a circle. Maybe your circles look lopsided or like potatoes. Here are 4 techniques to draw circles and maybe one of them will work for you.

Option 1: Place the heel of your hand on the paper. This will keep your hand in one place. Then, using just your fingers, lightly draw a circle over and over. Each time you go around, you are making another imperfect circle, but the total of all those imperfect ones should be one pretty good one.

Option 2: Lift your hand slightly so it is hovering just above the page. Make a circular motion using your shoulder and lower the pencil onto the page.

Option 3: Draw a square. Some artists can draw good squares even if they can't draw circles. Then draw an arc across each side from one corner to the next. You only have to draw a quarter of a circle at a time this way.

Option 4: Use a tool like a circle stencil or a compass. They make perfect circles every time.

A. Draw a circle about the same size as the example. Then draw a vertical line that divides your circle into two equal halves. Draw a horizontal line that cuts the circle in half the other way.

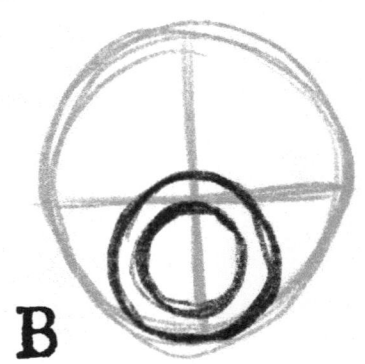

B. Begin on the dog's snout. Draw a smaller circle that rests in the lower half of the head circle. Inside of that new circle draw another, even smaller, circle. We will call these the outer snout circle and the inner snout circle. The inner one will become the dog's nose.

C. In this step we flatten out the head and add two circles for the eyes. Notice where those eye circles sit. They are touching the outer snout circle and are closer to the horizontal line than they are to the vertical line.

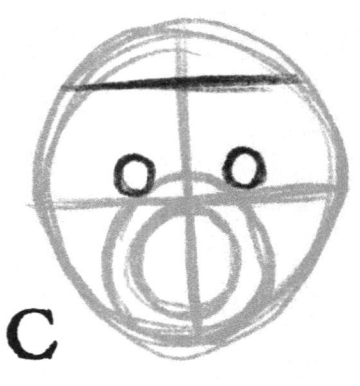

D. Where we flattened the head two corners were formed. These corners are where the ears will spring from. The ears go up, make a quick turn and come back down on the side of the head. Also in this step, we will draw a straight line down the middle of the inner snout circle. And halfway down that new line, draw a short horizontal line.

Drawing Dogs Tutorials and Sketchbook — THE SELTZER METHOD

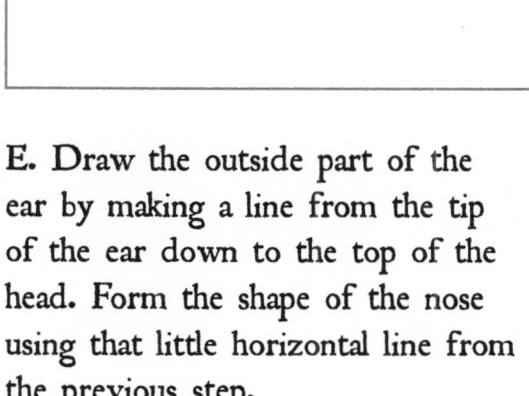

E. Draw the outside part of the ear by making a line from the tip of the ear down to the top of the head. Form the shape of the nose using that little horizontal line from the previous step.

F. The lips are formed by making a curved line from the bottom of the nose, down through the snout circles. When you get to the edge of the outer snout circle, flip the curve over.

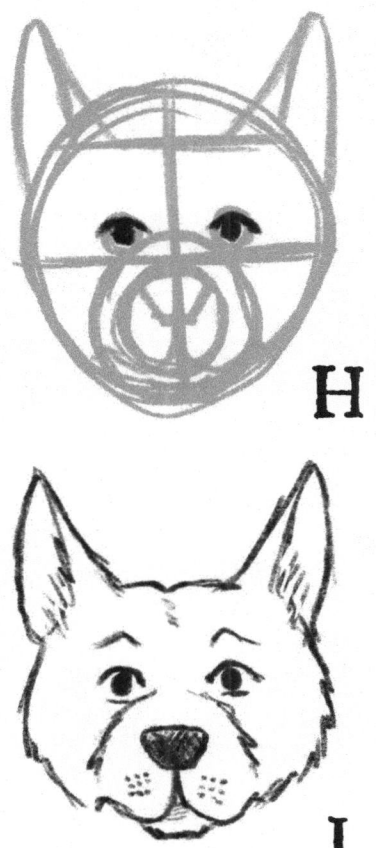

G. Draw the opposite lip and add a little chin below.

H. Make simple eyes with a dot and curved lid line.

I. Finish the drawing by erasing unneeded lines and adding a bold contour line. The contour line should be a little jagged to give the viewer a sense of fur.

Drawing Dogs Tutorials and Sketchbook — THE Seltzer METHOD

Drawing a dog's head from the side

A

B

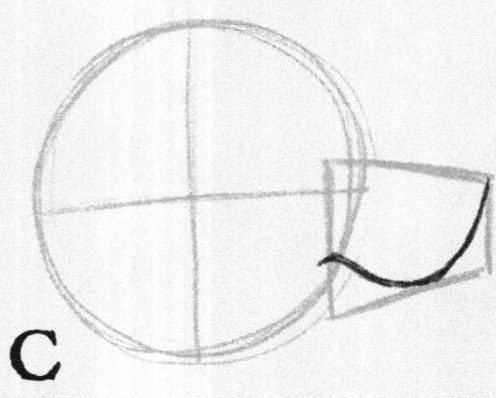
C

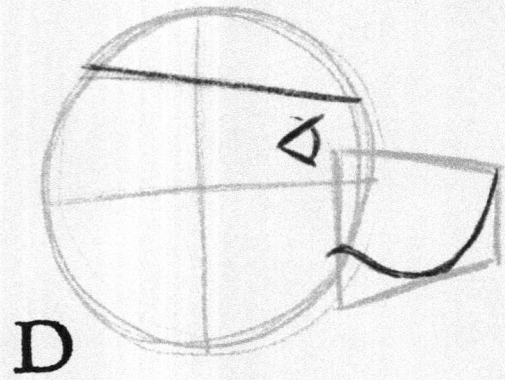
D

A. Draw a circle about the same size as the example. Then draw a vertical line that divides your circle into two equal halves. Draw a horizontal line that cuts the circle in half the other way.

B. Begin on the dog's snout. Use a trapezoid, like the one shown, and place it on one side of the circle. It should be placed below the center of the circle and overlap the circle a small amount.

C. From the top outer corner of the trapezoid, begin a curve that sweeps down and towards the circle. When you reach the inner edge of the trapezoid, flip the curve and stop. This is the line of the mouth. The trapezoid beneath this line will not be needed again and can be erased.

D. Add the eye by placing a curve inside an angle. The line across the top of the snout will point at the eye. This will not always be the case for every breed. Next, flatten the top of the head, but when you do, tilt it forward towards the snout. Leave just a little room between the eye and this new line.

Drawing Dogs Tutorials and Sketchbook — THE seltzer METHOD

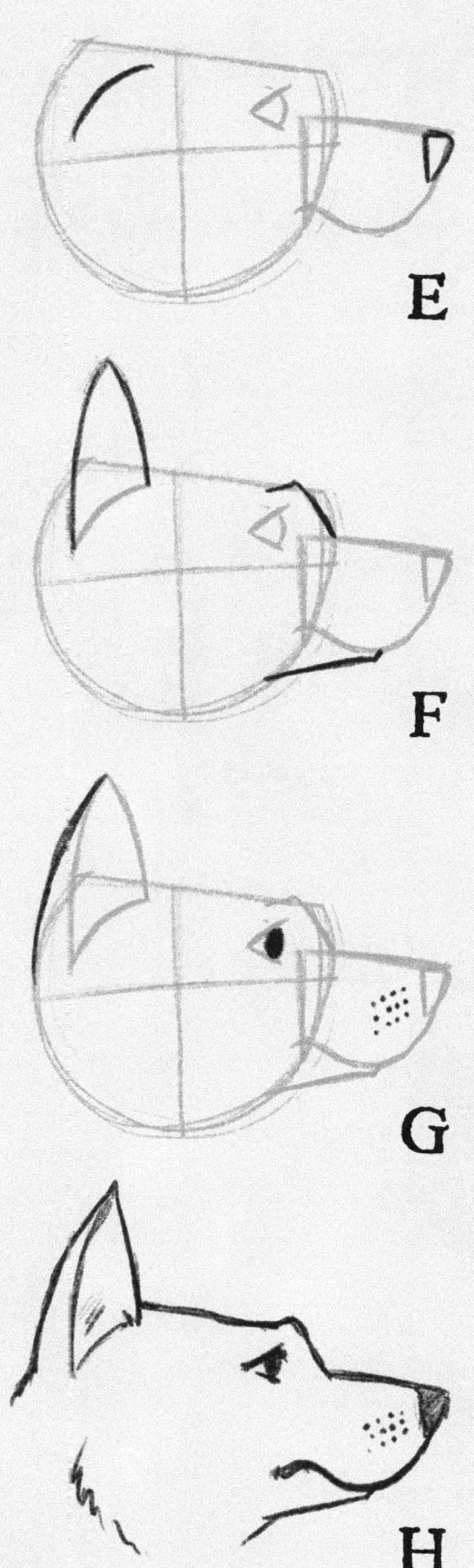

E. The tip of the snout is obviously where the nose belongs. Mark out an area for it that looks good to you. In this step we will also mark the ear arc. This arc is where the ear connects to the head. The arc is centered in the back upper quadrant of the head. Although the different breeds will have a wide variety of ear shapes, this arc remains the same.

F. The ear is a tall arch that begins at one side of the ear arch and ends at the other side. Next, connect the top of the head to the snout, giving a slight ridge on top where an eyebrow might be. We can also add in the dog's lower jaw. It is a straight line that extends to lowest point of the lip's curve.

G. Add in the colored part of the eye. There isn't much white visible in a dog's eye. The colored part should take up most of the space. We can also add the back of the ear by drawing a curve from the tip of the ear down to the back of the head. Let's also add in the whisker marks. These are three or four lines of dots on the snout.

H. Finally, it is time to erase any unneeded lines and add our final contour line. Everything we have done so far should be thought of as a rough draft. Go over these lines with a stronger hand and bring it all together.

Drawing a dog's body from the side

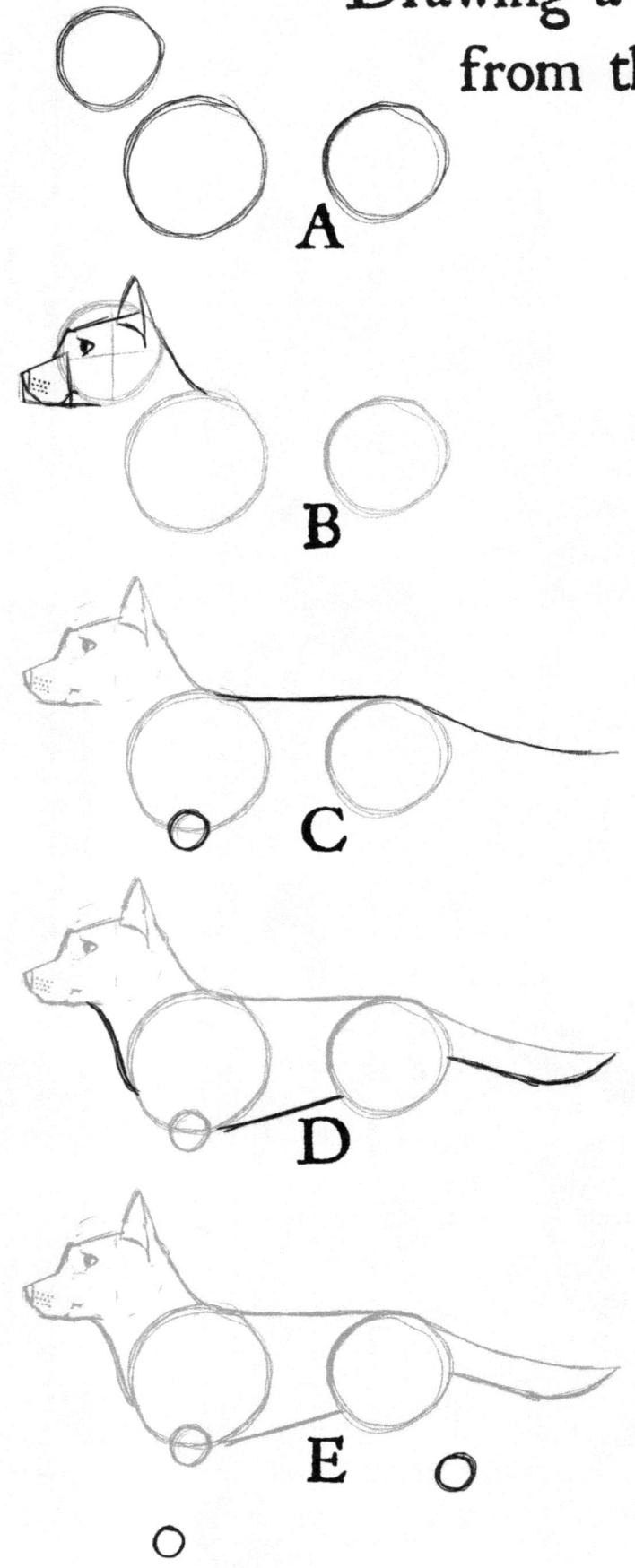

A. The dog's body starts as three circle; head, chest, and hip. The chest is the largest of the three. Distances between these circles and their relative sizes will vary by breed.

B. Draw the head (see previous page.) Connect the back of the head to the top of the chest circle. This is the beginning of the backbone.

C. Continue the backbone from the chest circle to the hip circle and then onward to form the tail. Add a small circle at the bottom of the chest circle. This will be the dog's elbow.

D. Connect the lower jaw to the front of the chest. Connect the bottom of the chest to the hip circle, almost to the bottom of the hip circle but not quite. Also, flesh out the tail.

E. Add a smaller circle beneath the elbow. This will be the wrist joint. Notice that it is slightly in front of the elbow. You will also add a joint for the hind leg. This joint is called the hock and is common in most four legged mammals. The hock is located just behind the hip circle and a bit below. The position will vary by breed.

F. Connect the elbow and wrist joints with straight lines. Connect the hip circle and hock joint with curved lines as shown in diagram F on the next page.

Drawing Dogs Tutorials and Sketchbook — THE seltzer METHOD

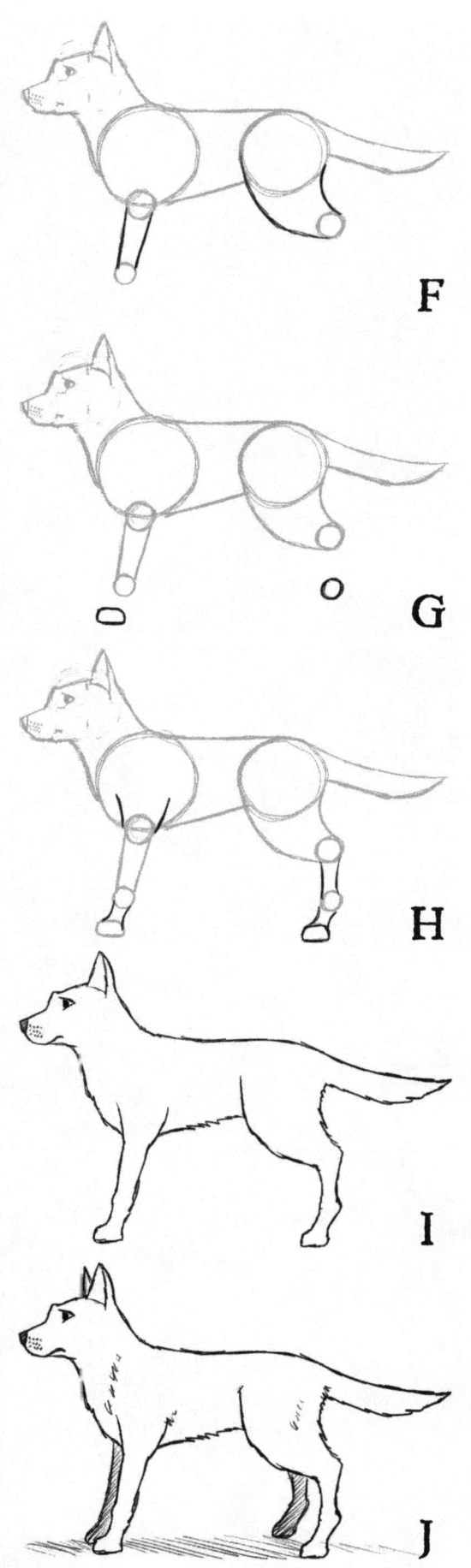

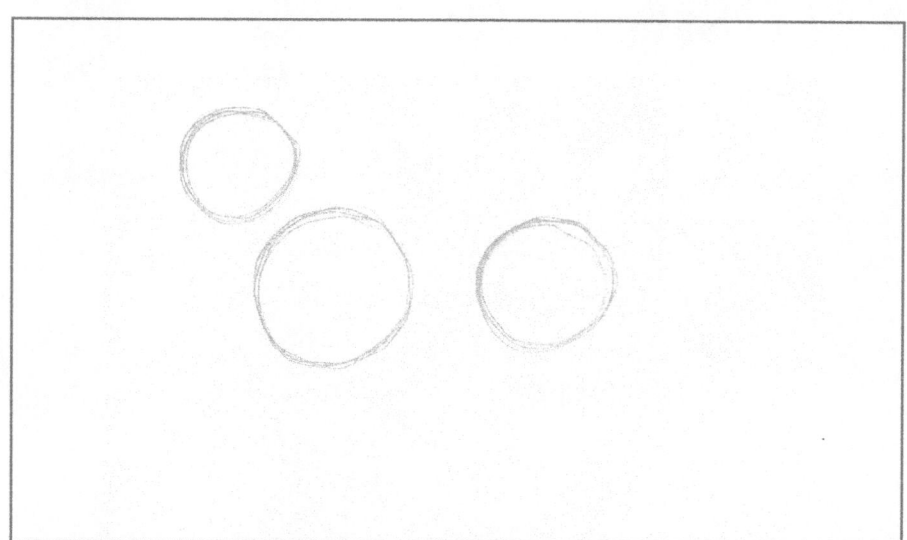

G. Add a lower ankle joint for the hind leg. Add a paw for the front leg shaped like a rounded rectangle.

H. Add a paw to the hind leg and connect the paws and joints using concave lines (lines that bend inward.) For the upper arm add lines from the elbow that vanish upward into the dog's chest.

I. Now erase any pencil lines that don't belong. Many of the circles made along the way will be partially erased on this step. Make the contour line. A "contour" is a line that runs along the outside edge of something. This line should be stronger than your sketch lines. The character of this line will tell the viewer about the fur in that area. A smooth line gives the feeling of short fur. Jagged lines give the feeling of longer fur.

J. Draw in the opposite side limbs and ear. The front paws are not as wide apart as the back paws. Once you have sketched them in the way you like them, add a shadow to them. This will downplay them visually. They need to be there but we don't want to draw attention to them. You can add a shadow on the ground which will help anchor your dog to the page. Also, add some details into the fur to indicate where fur is longer or where there are shadows made by the fur. Don't overdo it. Just a few well-placed marks can convey a lot.

Drawing Dogs
Tutorials and Sketchbook

THE Seltzer METHOD

Drawing in 3 Dimensions

We live in a 3-dimensional world so drawing in three dimensions should be easy. Of course, that isn't true. The reason is because we are drawing on a 2-dimensional surface. You would probably have an easier time sculpting a dog's head from clay than drawing one on paper.

Overcoming this limitation is as simple as changing our mindset. Instead of thinking in terms of shapes like circles and triangles, we instead need to think about forms like spheres and cones. For example, the dog's head can be reduced to two forms; a sphere and a cup. The cup is just a cone that has had it's tip cut off. The sphere represents the dog's cranium (skull) and the cup is the snout. Eyes, ears, and nose can then be added on.

Practice drawing these forms on the opposite page. What happens if you point the dog's head in a different direction? How does the cup change? Try changing the size of the cup.

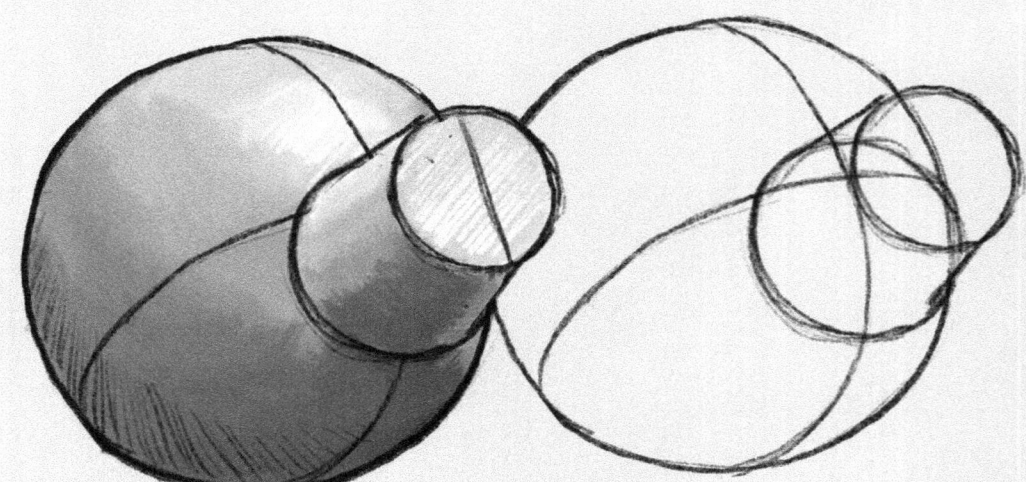

Drawing Dogs
Tutorials and Sketchbook

THE SELTZER METHOD

Drawing in 3 Dimensions
continued

We can now apply this idea to the whole body. The chest and hip circles become spheres. The joints of the legs are smaller spheres. When you connect all these together, you end up with a fairly accurate 3D model of a dog.

On the sketch below, connect the spheres together using the lines shown in the examples. Don't worry about the features of the head at this stage. As you proceed through this book you will have many opportunities to draw the head from a variety of angles. Instead, focus on understanding how the dog exists in space.

In the space provided on the next page, try drawing this simple dog from a slightly different angle. Rotate it a little to the left or to the right. Can you point the head in a different direction?

Drawing Dogs
Tutorials and Sketchbook

THE seltzer METHOD

Bernese Mountain Dog

First noted as part of Roman armies, the Mountain Dog has filled many roles. It has been used to herd, to guard, and even as a draft animal, pulling carts. The Bernese Mountain Dog and its similar cousins are most common in the snowy Swiss Alps.

Step 1

Step 2

Step 3

Step 4

Step 5

Step 6

Drawing Dogs
Tutorials and Sketchbook

THE SELTZER METHOD

Bernese Mountain Dog

Step 1
Step 2
Step 3
Step 4
Step 5

Bernese Mountain Dogs are large, with heavy bones and voluminous fur. They have a distinctive color pattern made of white, black, and reddish-brown. Getting that pattern correct is essential for viewers to recognize the breed in your drawing.

Drawing Dogs
Tutorials and Sketchbook

THE Seltzer METHOD

Drawing Dogs Tutorials and Sketchbook — THE SELTZER METHOD

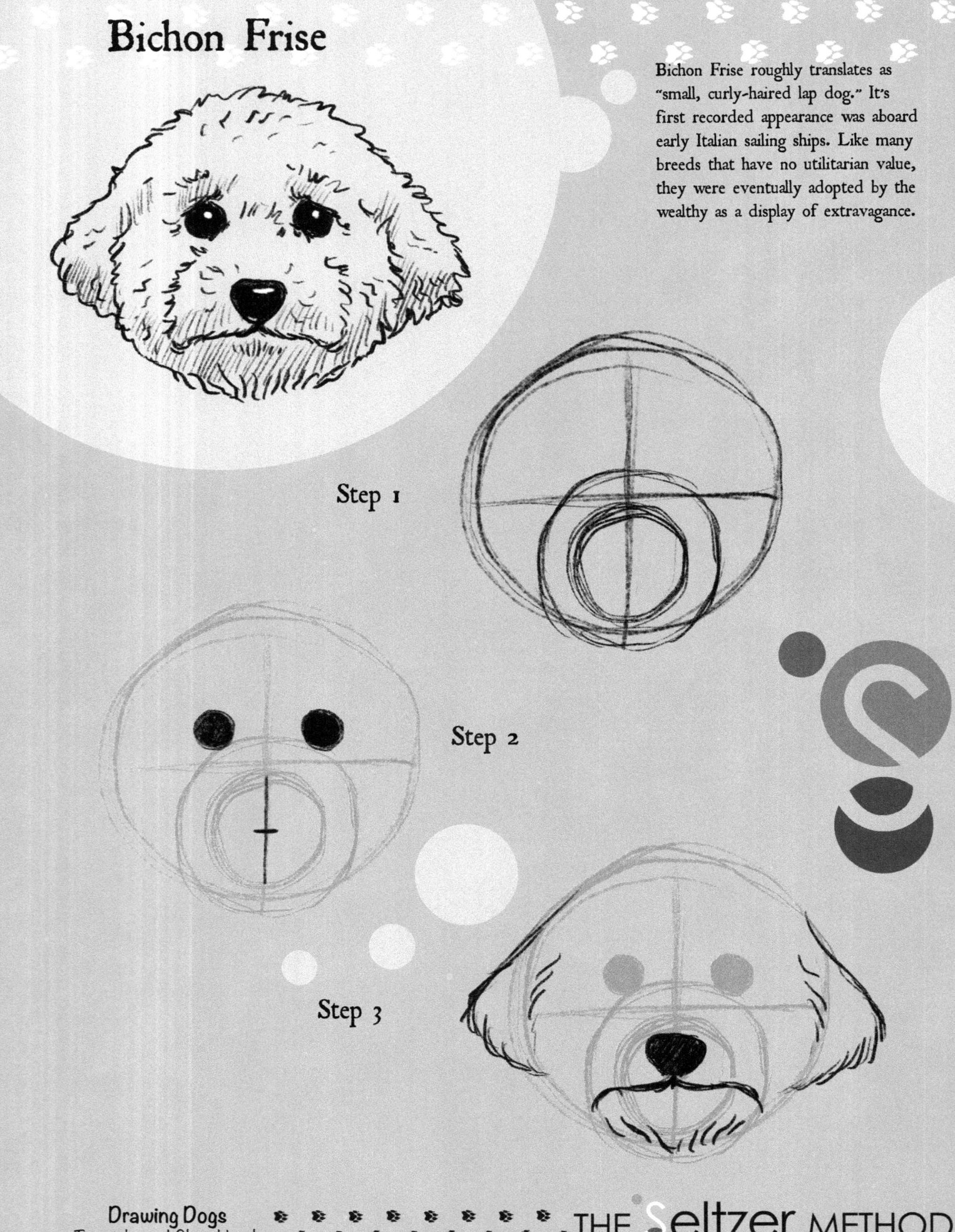

Bichon Frise

Bichon Frise roughly translates as "small, curly-haired lap dog." It's first recorded appearance was aboard early Italian sailing ships. Like many breeds that have no utilitarian value, they were eventually adopted by the wealthy as a display of extravagance.

Step 1

Step 2

Step 3

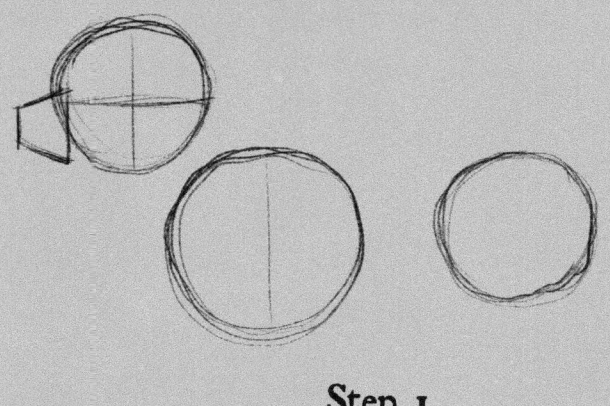
Step 1

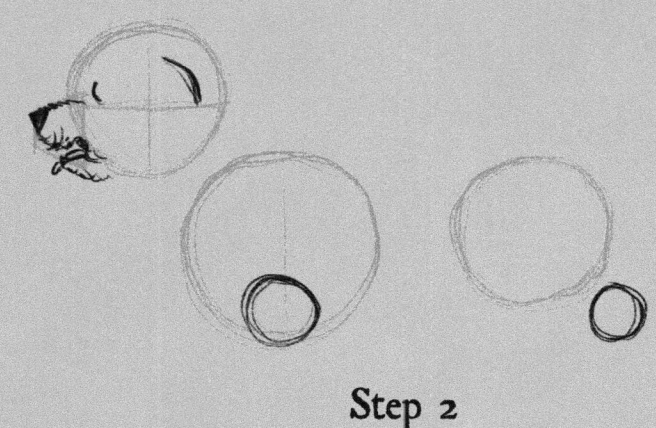
Step 2

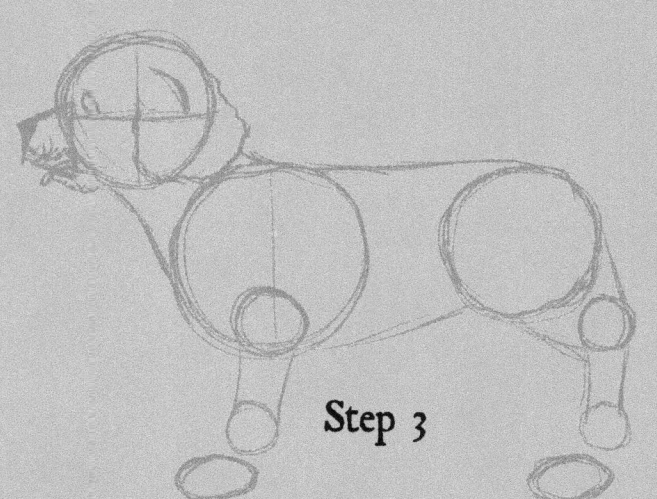
Step 3

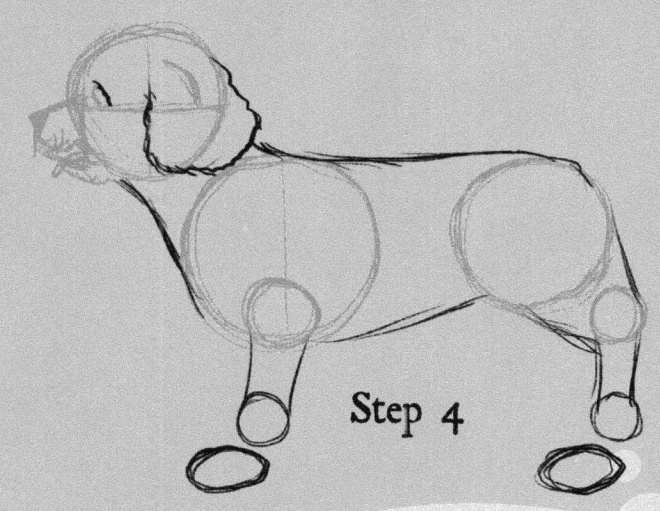
Step 4

Bichon Frise

The Bichon Frise has a short snout but an otherwise classical body. Like other water dogs, they have hair, not fur, which must be brushed and trimmed. Note the contour line around the edges of the dog that indicate the texture of the fur. In the final steps, that contour line is broken into short, wavy segments.

Bloodhound

The Bloodhound was developed during the Dark Ages in Europe to track deer, boar, and human fugitives by scent over long distances. They have a keen sense of smell and also the instinct to follow scent trails.

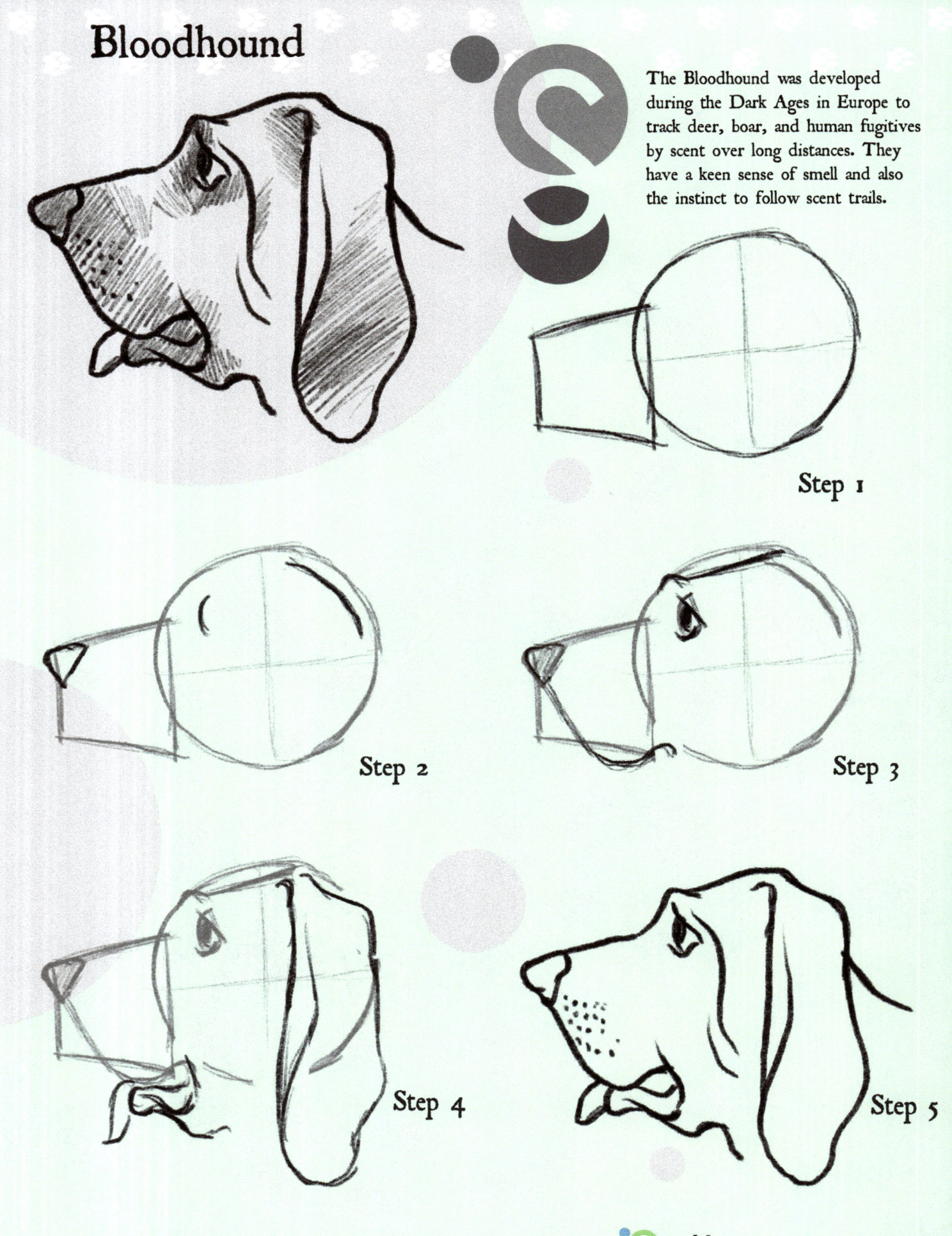

Step 1

Step 2

Step 3

Step 4

Step 5

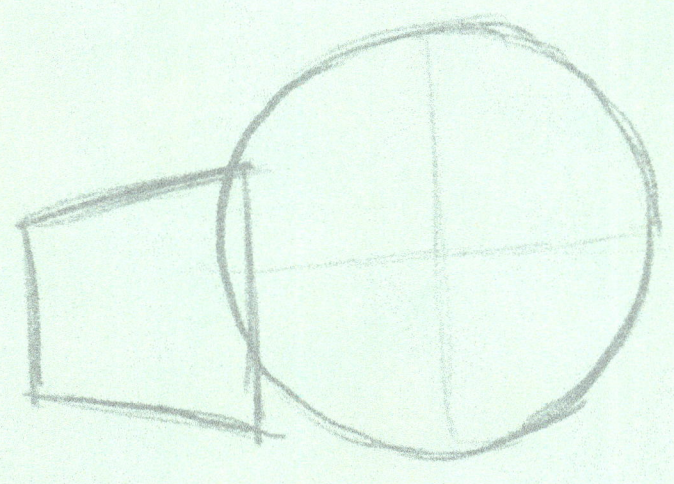

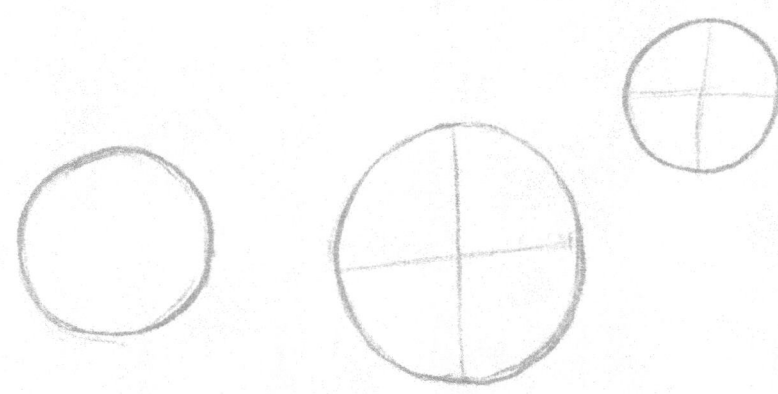

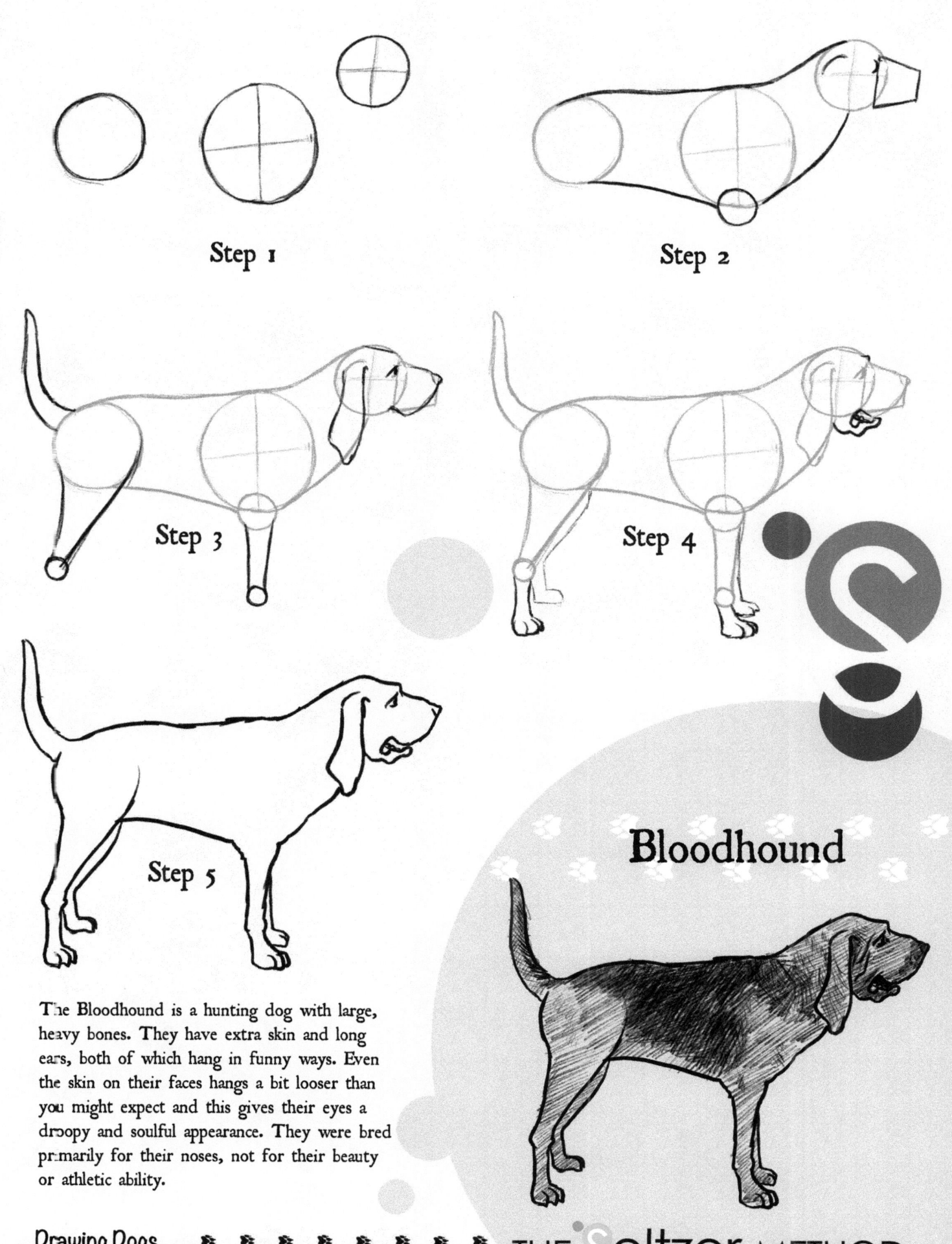

Step 1

Step 2

Step 3

Step 4

Step 5

Bloodhound

The Bloodhound is a hunting dog with large, heavy bones. They have extra skin and long ears, both of which hang in funny ways. Even the skin on their faces hangs a bit looser than you might expect and this gives their eyes a droopy and soulful appearance. They were bred primarily for their noses, not for their beauty or athletic ability.

Drawing Dogs Tutorials and Sketchbook

THE Seltzer METHOD

Drawing Dogs
Tutorials and Sketchbook

THE Seltzer METHOD

35

Chihuahua

The Chihuahua is native to the Americas. The earliest accounts from European explorers describe how the Aztecs raised them for food. Ancient relics show that these tiny dogs were prevalent throughout Central America and many parts of North America.

Step 1

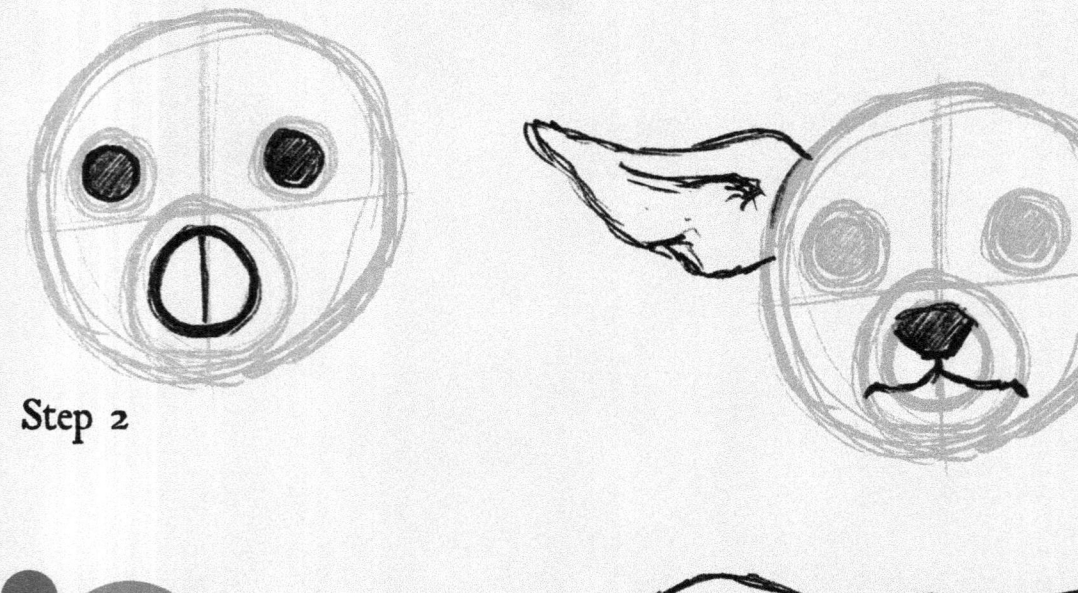

Step 2

Step 3

Step 4

Drawing Dogs
Tutorials and Sketchbook

THE SELTZER METHOD

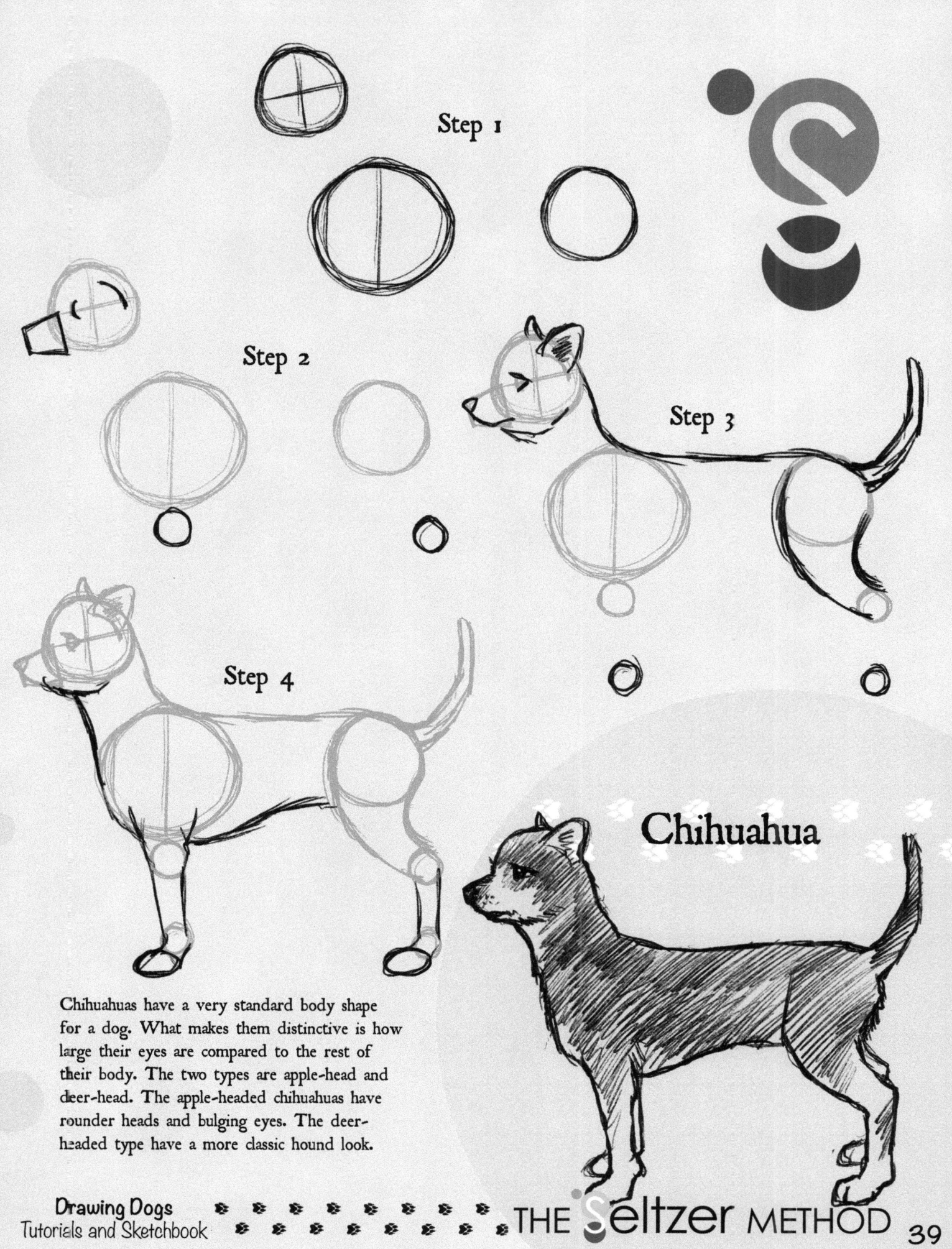

Drawing Dogs Tutorials and Sketchbook — THE Seltzer METHOD

Drawing Dogs
Tutorials and Sketchbook

THE Seltzer METHOD

43

Collie

Collies are a category of herding dogs. The dog pictured here is called a Rough Collie. It is a sheep-herding dog bred in Scotland in the 1800s. Their heavy, double-layered coat may keep them warm but requires frequent brushing.

Step 1 Step 2 Step 3 Step 4

Drawing Dogs Tutorials and Sketchbook • THE SELTZER METHOD

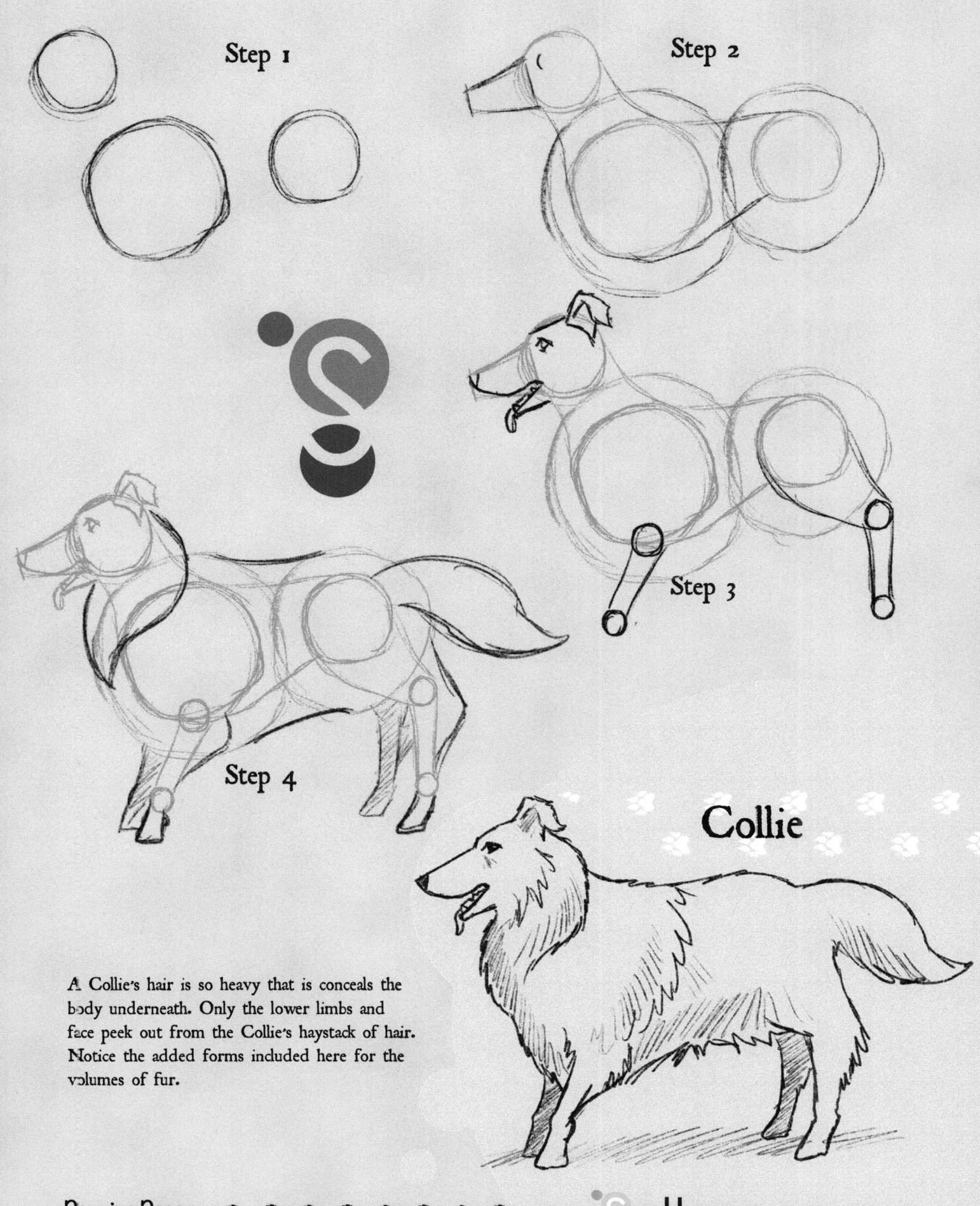

Drawing Dogs
Tutorials and Sketchbook

THE seltzer METHOD

Drawing Dogs
Tutorials and Sketchbook

THE seltzer METHOD
51

Dachshund

The Dachshund, which translates as badger dog, was bred to hunt badgers and other burrowing animals. They have short, powerful legs for digging and long narrow bodies that can get into tunnels. They are commonly known as wiener dogs or sausage dogs because of their shape and also their association with Germany.

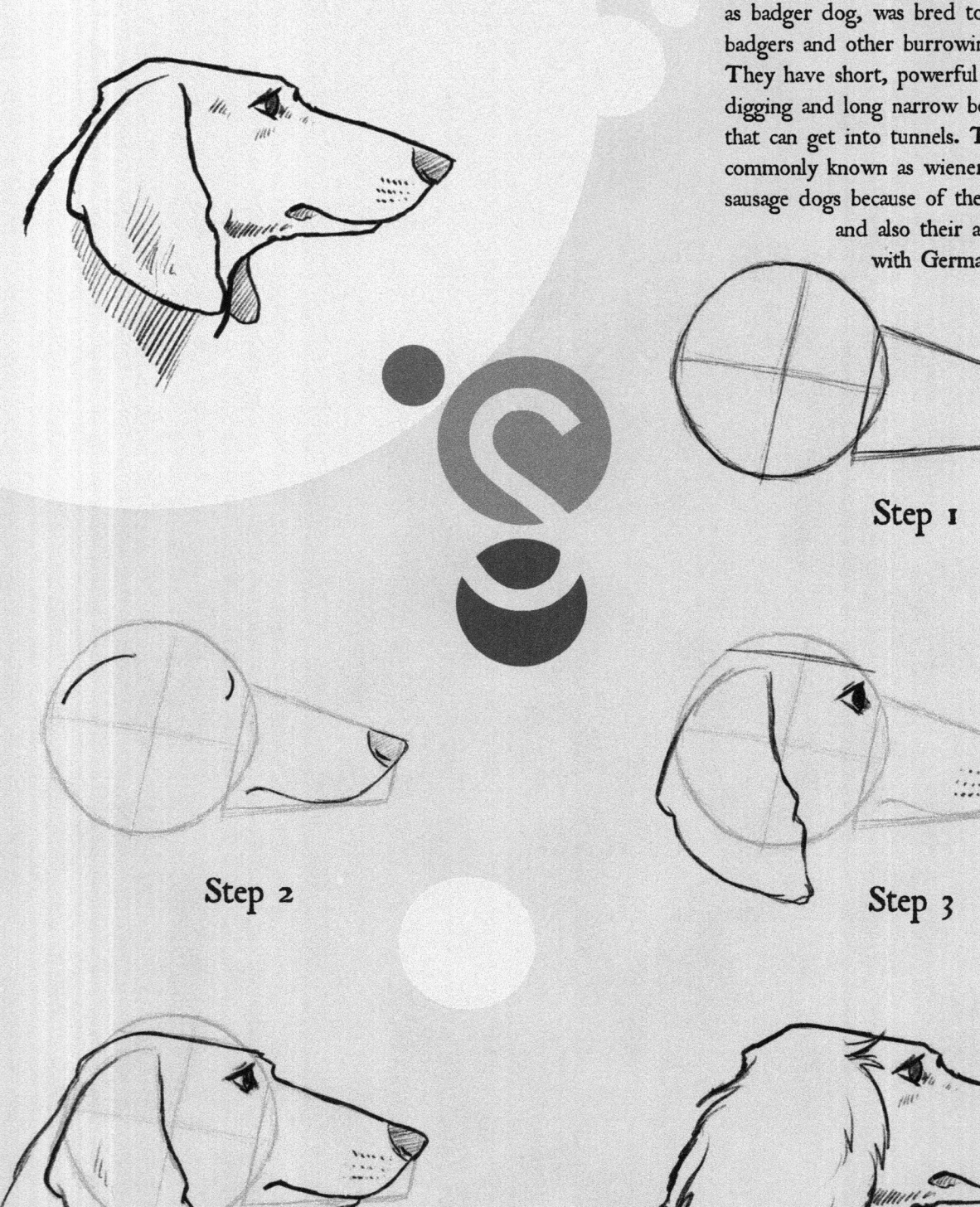

Step 1

Step 2

Step 3

Step 4

Dachshund breeds can have short hair, wiry hair, or long hair.

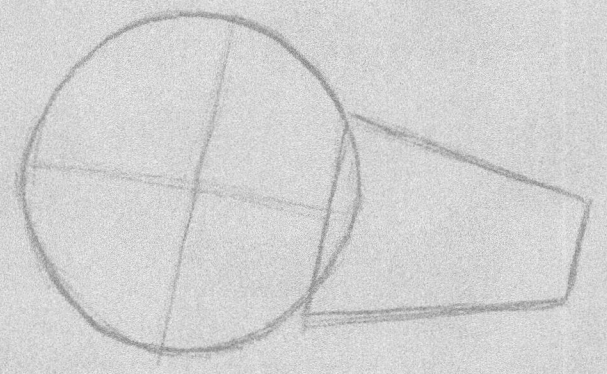

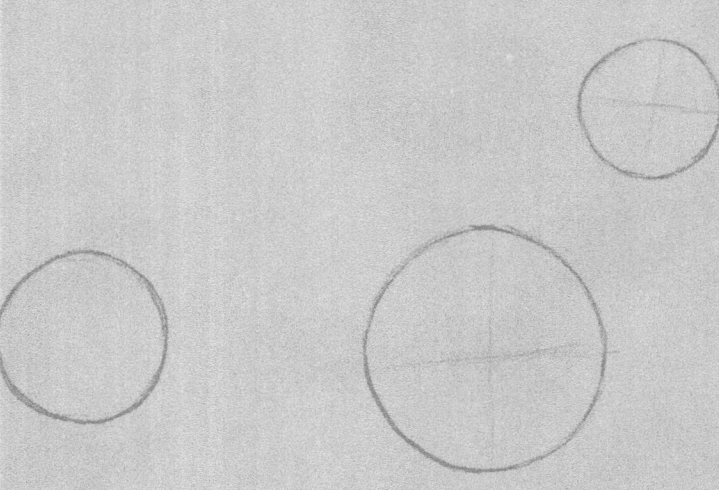

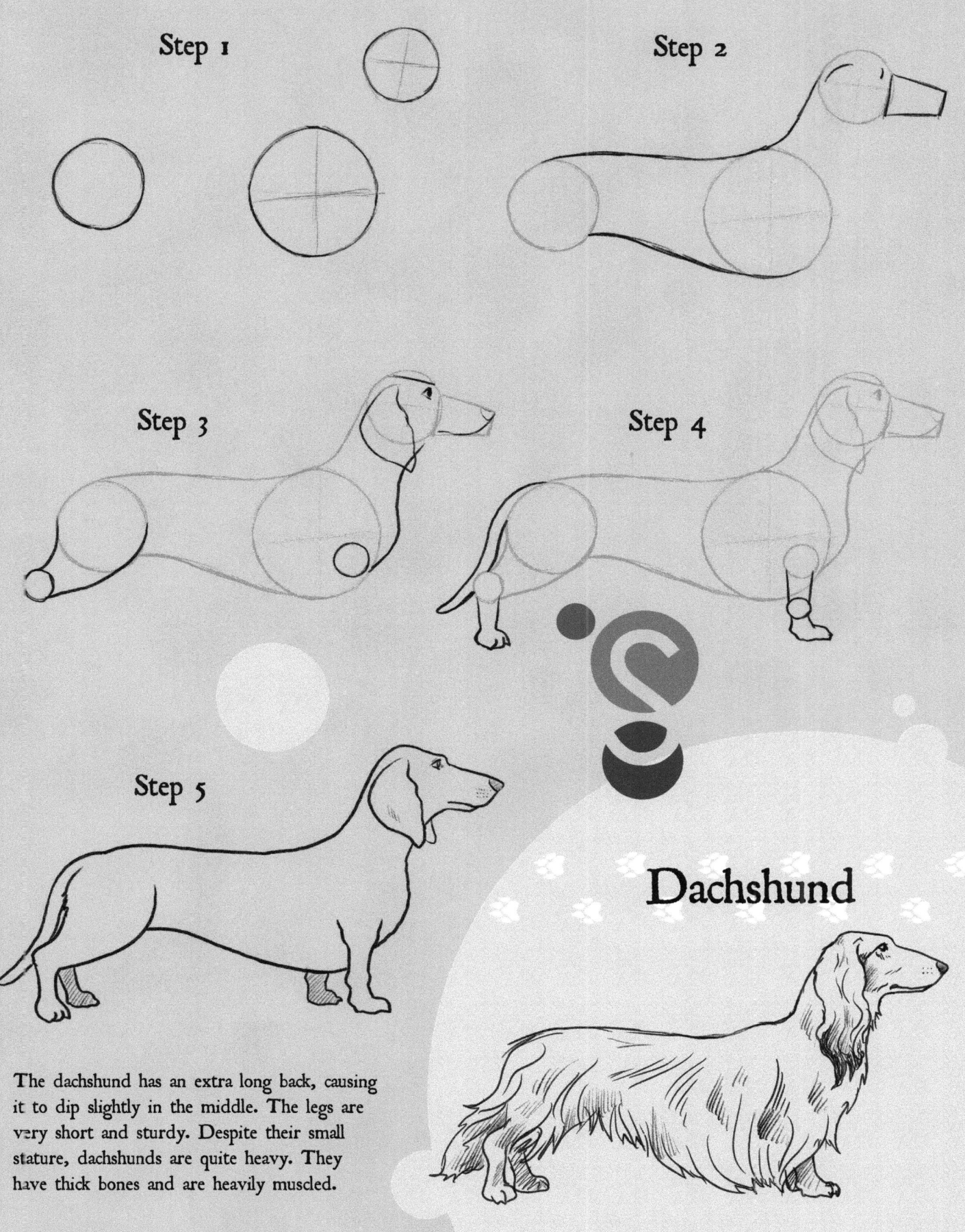

Step 1

Step 2

Step 3

Step 4

Step 5

Dachshund

The dachshund has an extra long back, causing it to dip slightly in the middle. The legs are very short and sturdy. Despite their small stature, dachshunds are quite heavy. They have thick bones and are heavily muscled.

French Bulldog

The French Bulldog is a combination of the big, strong bulldog and the fast, agile terrier. Unsuited to the role of either, the breed became a symbol of the leisure lifestyle of upper-class citizens in France.

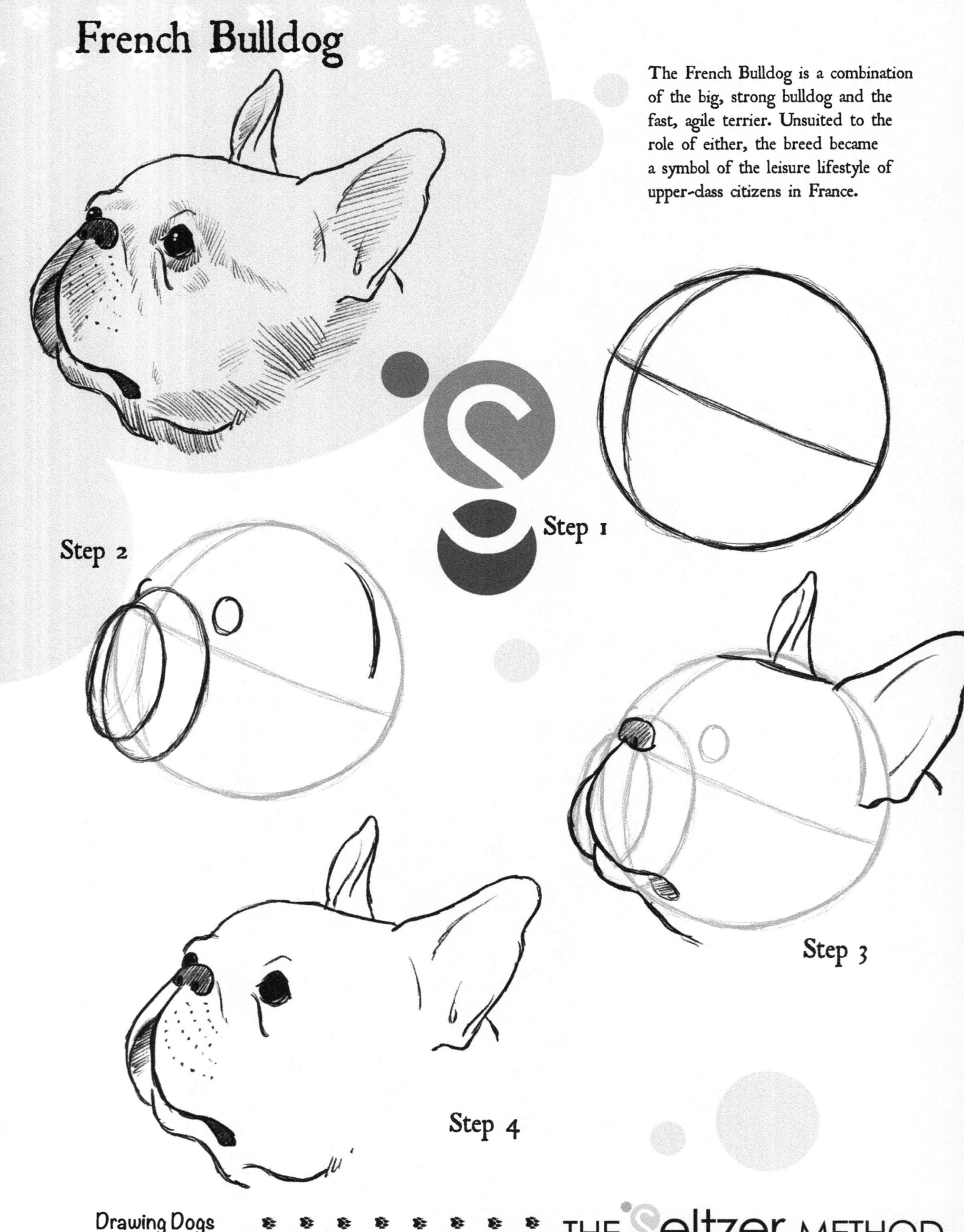

Step 1

Step 2

Step 3

Step 4

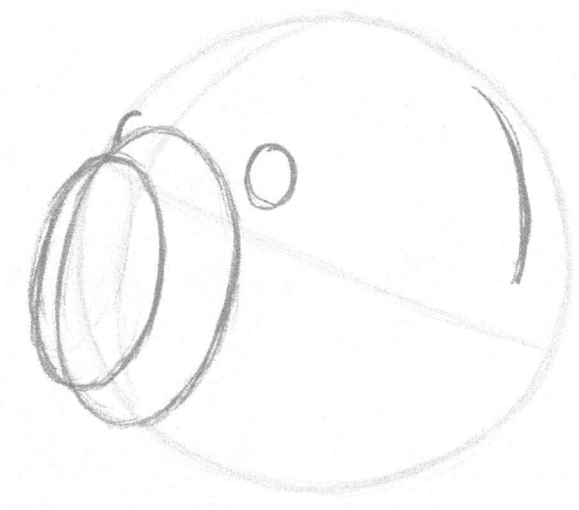

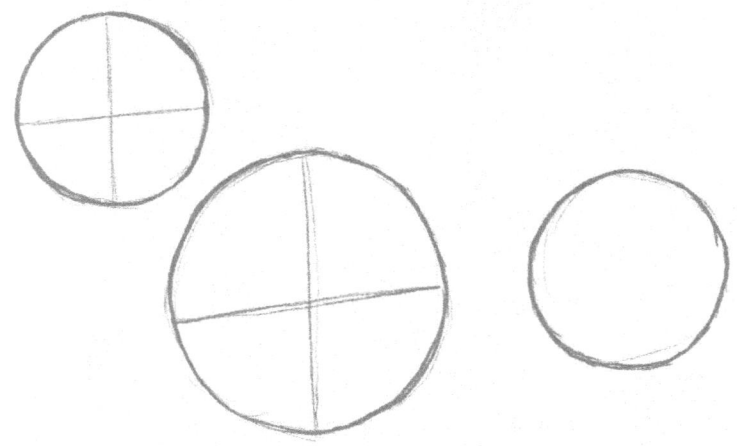

Drawing Dogs Tutorials and Sketchbook — THE Seltzer METHOD

German Shepherd

German Shepherds come from a long tradition of European sheep-herding dogs. In the late 1800s these dogs were selectively bred for intelligence and loyalty. A few wolves were mixed in, adding to the breed's wolf-life appearance.

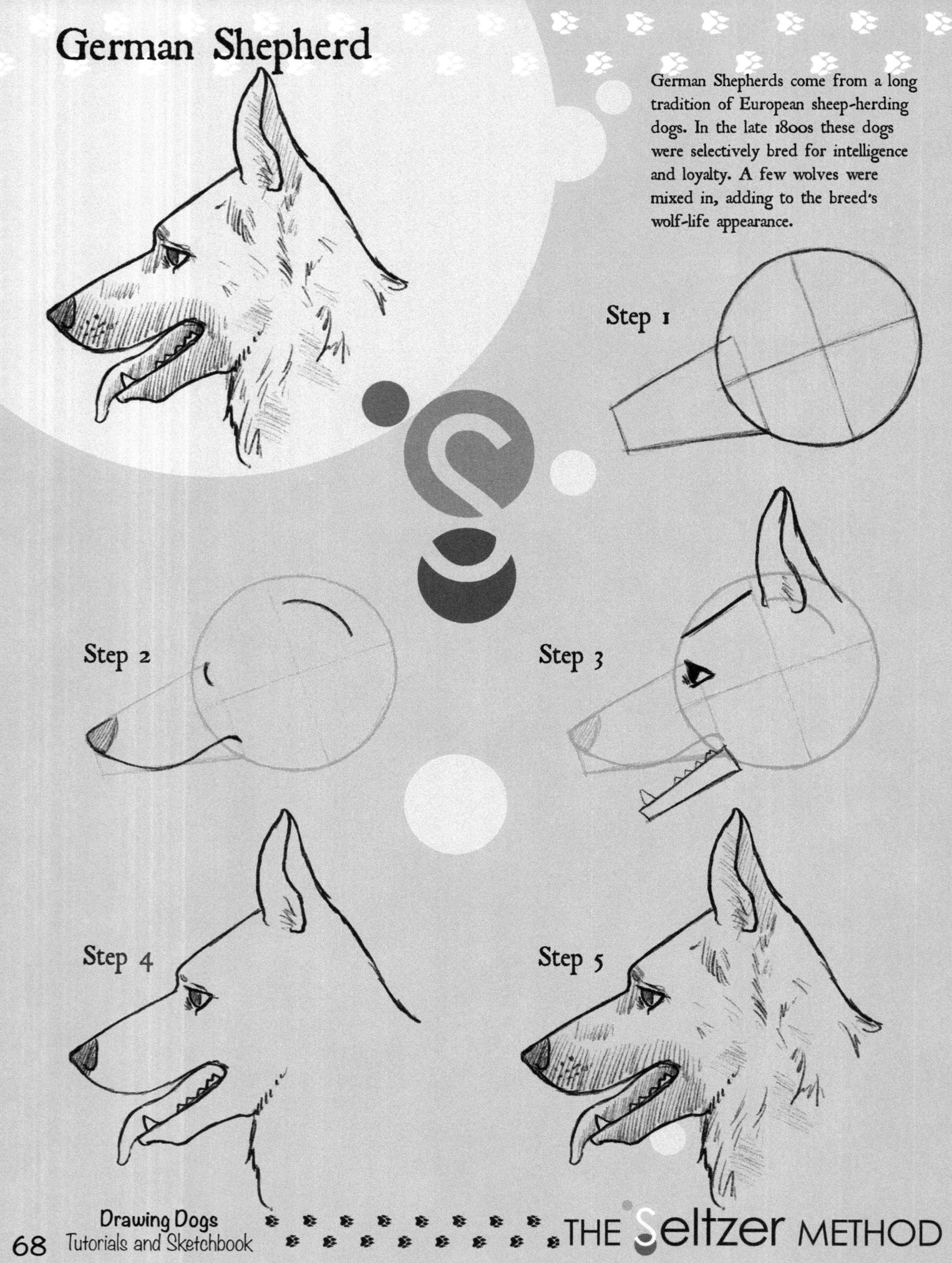

Step 1

Step 2

Step 3

Step 4

Step 5

Drawing Dogs Tutorials and Sketchbook

THE SELTZER METHOD

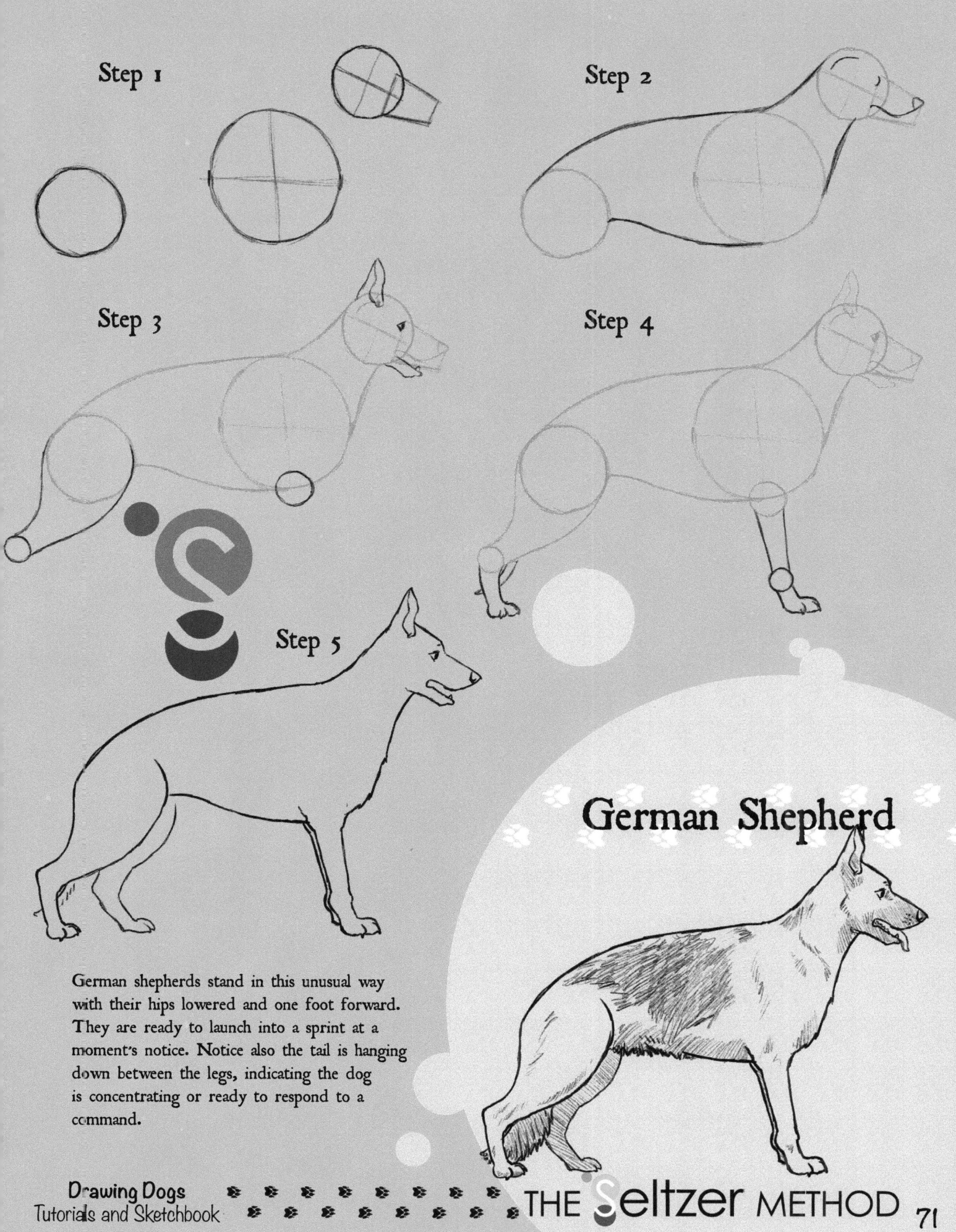

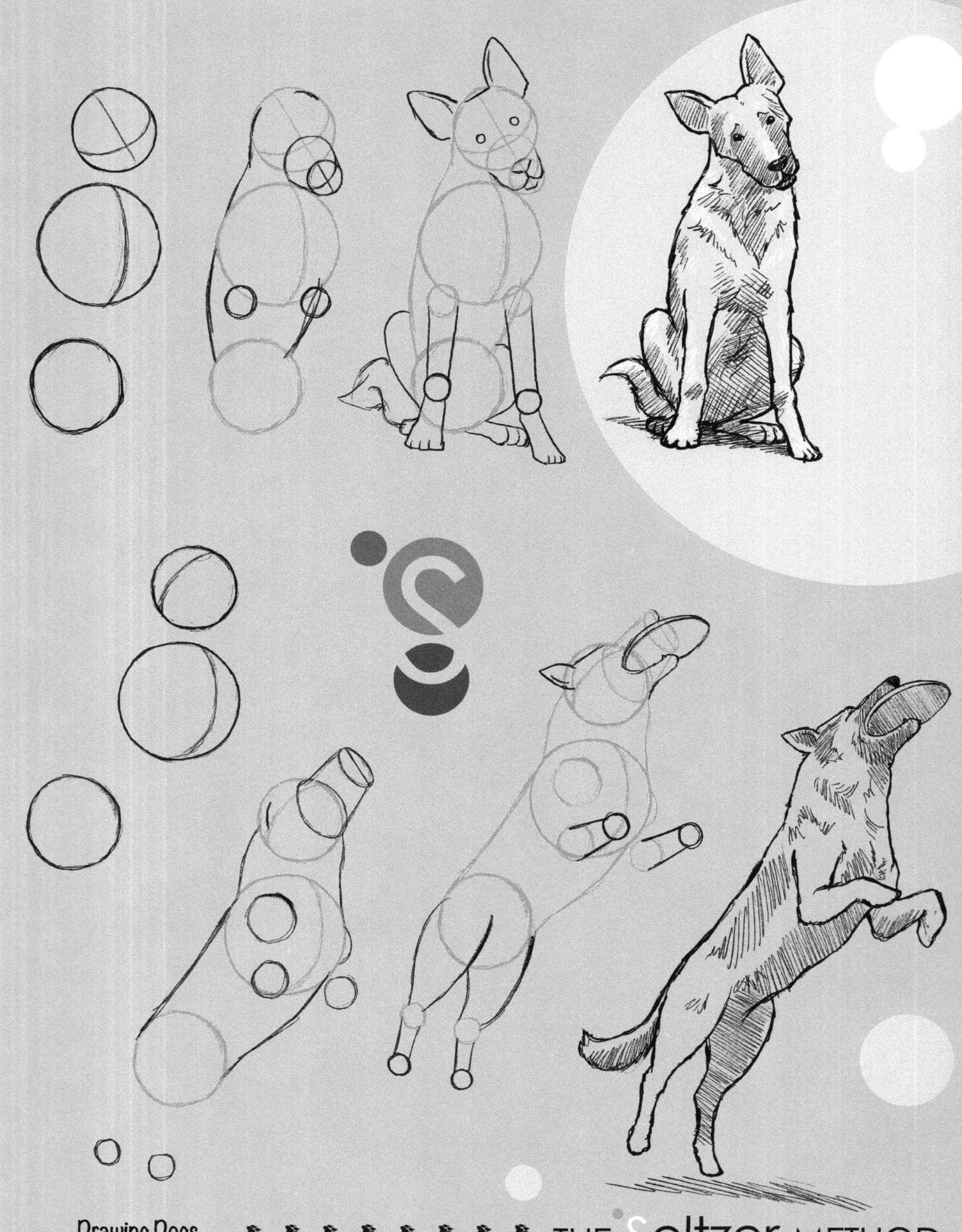

Drawing Dogs
Tutorials and Sketchbook

THE Seltzer METHOD

72

Drawing Dogs
Tutorials and Sketchbook   THE Seltzer METHOD

Great Dane

The Great Dane was bred fairly recently from other large hunting breeds. They have never been as useful as their ancestors but instead have served as status symbols of nobility.

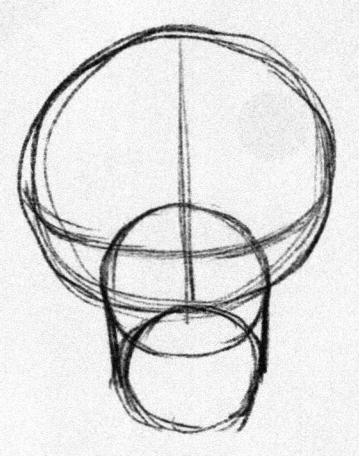
Step 1

Step 2

Step 4

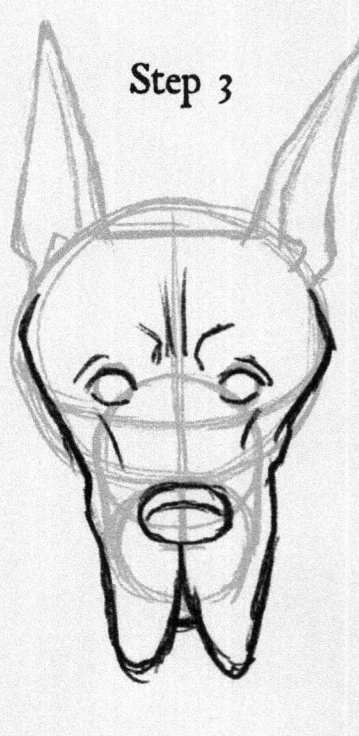
Step 3

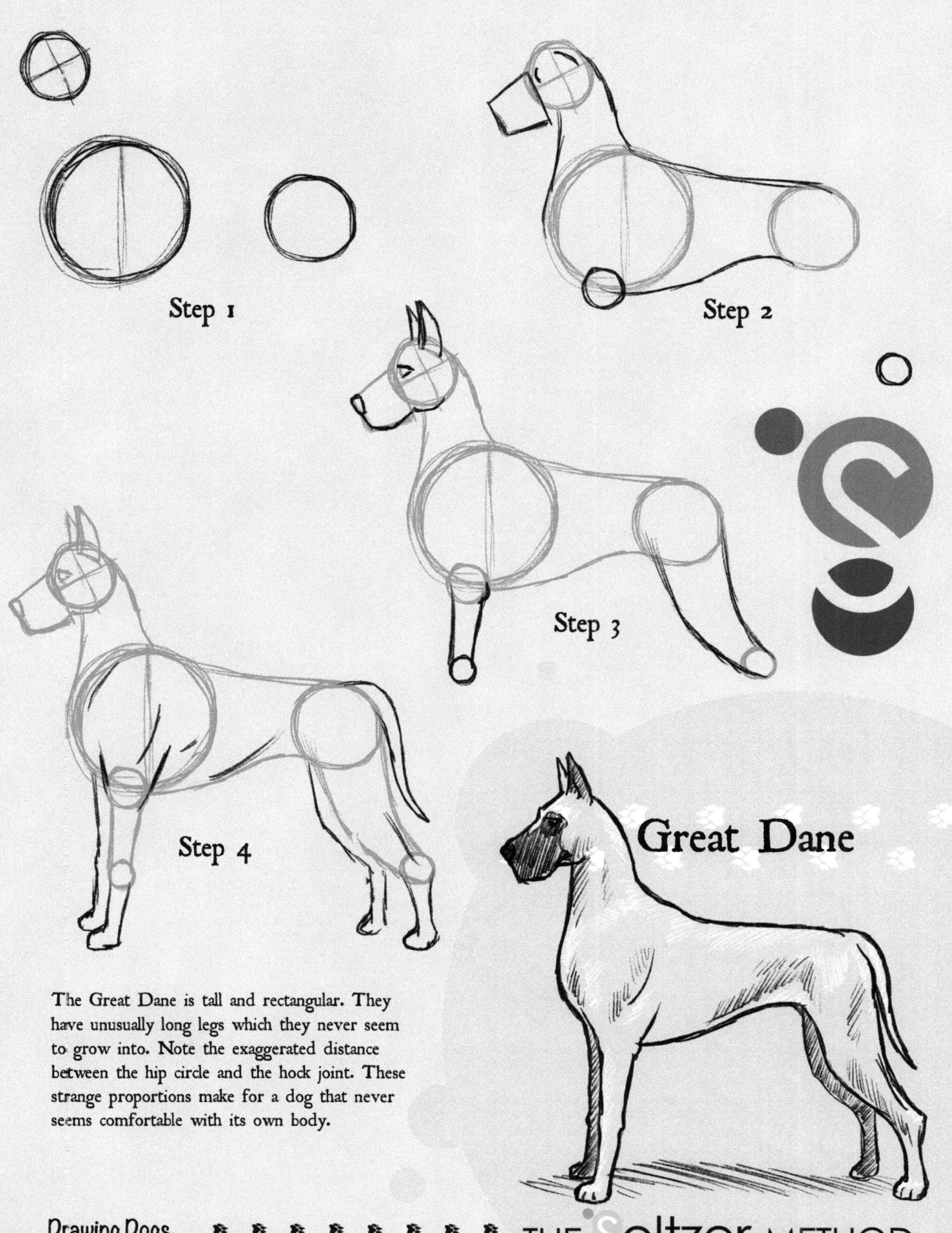

Step 1

Step 2

Step 3

Step 4

Great Dane

The Great Dane is tall and rectangular. They have unusually long legs which they never seem to grow into. Note the exaggerated distance between the hip circle and the hock joint. These strange proportions make for a dog that never seems comfortable with its own body.

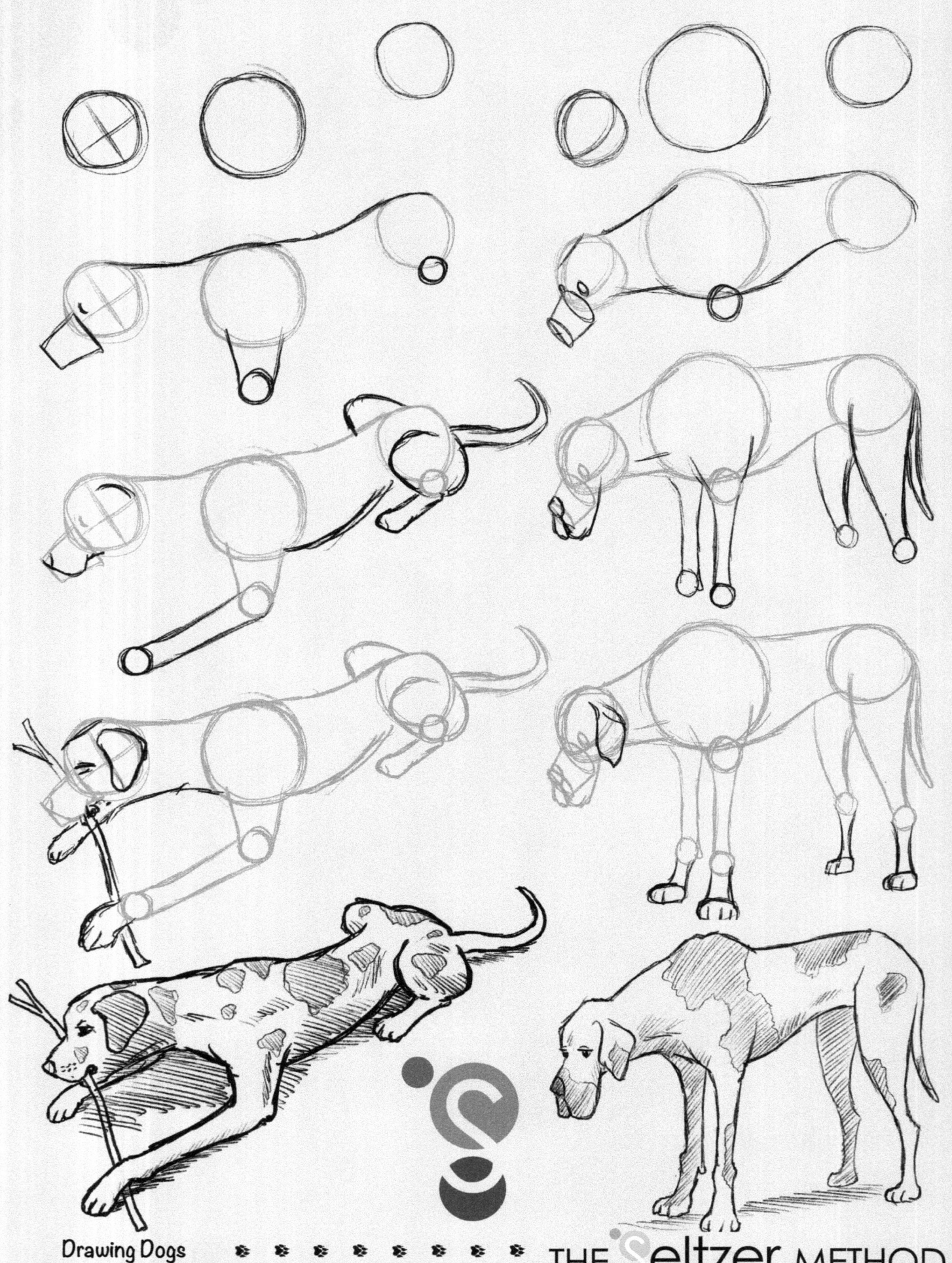

Drawing Dogs
Tutorials and Sketchbook

THE SELTZER METHOD

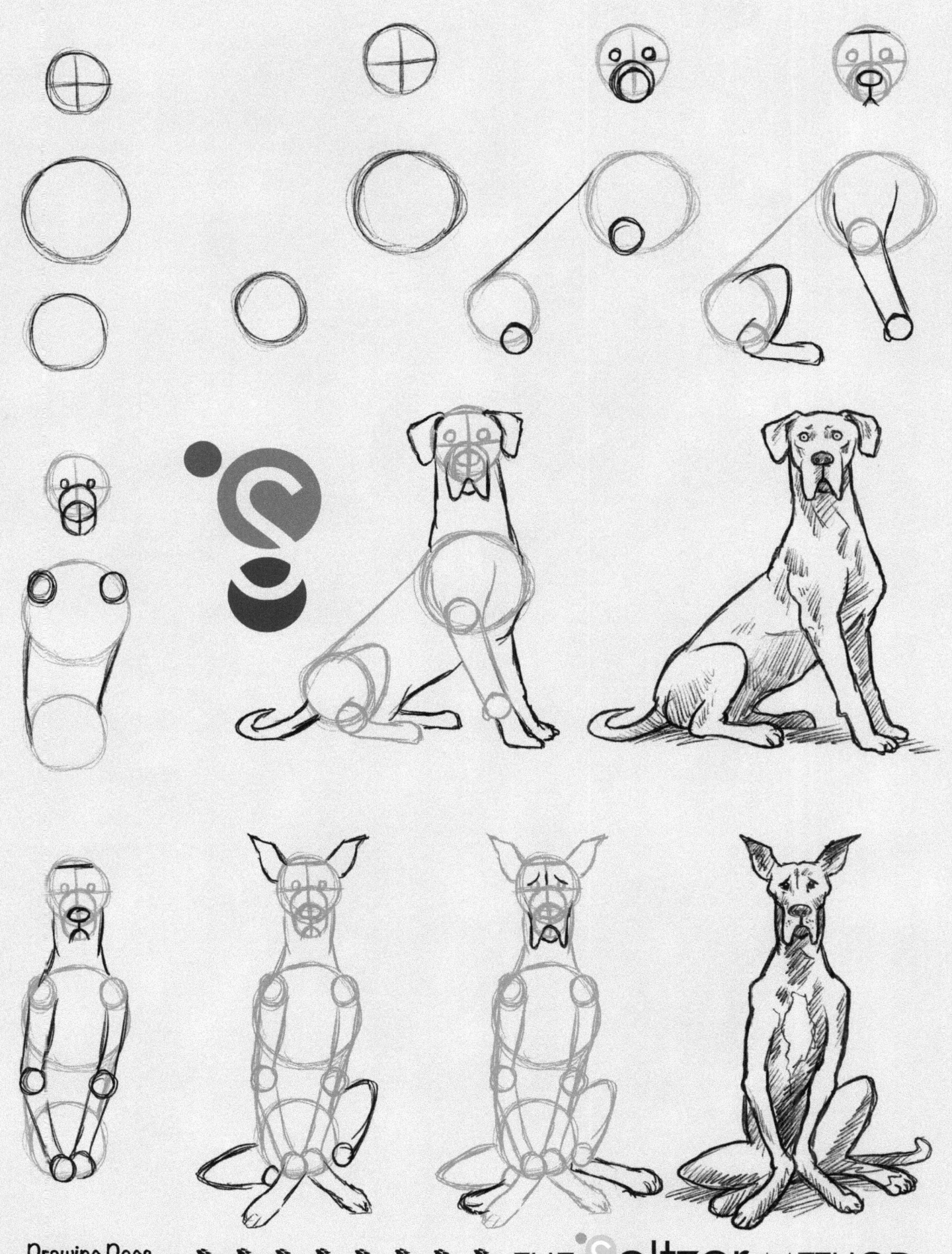

Golden Retriever

The Golden Retriever breed was created in the mid 1800s in Scotland. Using guns to hunt birds had become popular and a dog was needed that could fetch the downed birds from both water and land.

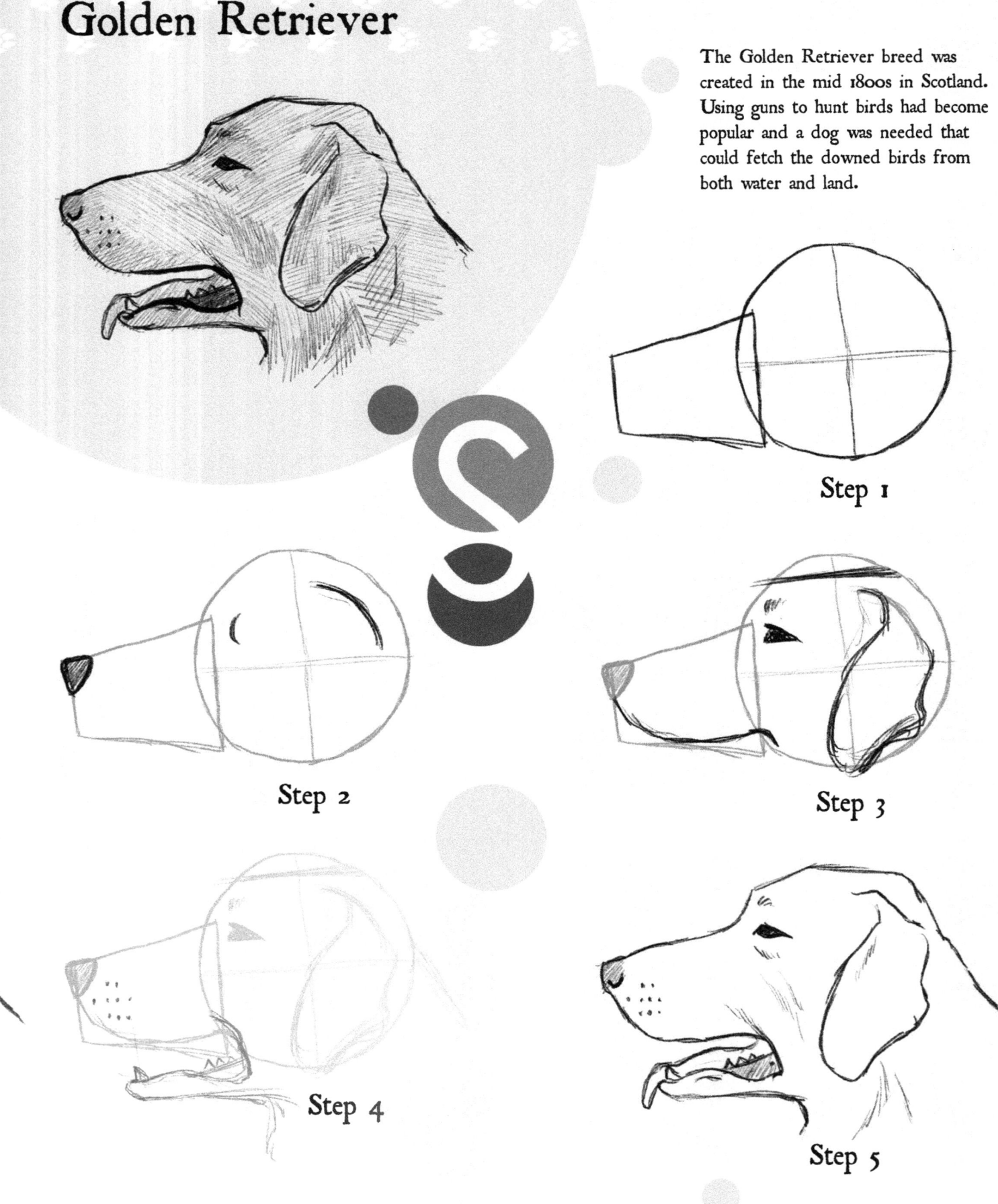

Step 1

Step 2

Step 3

Step 4

Step 5

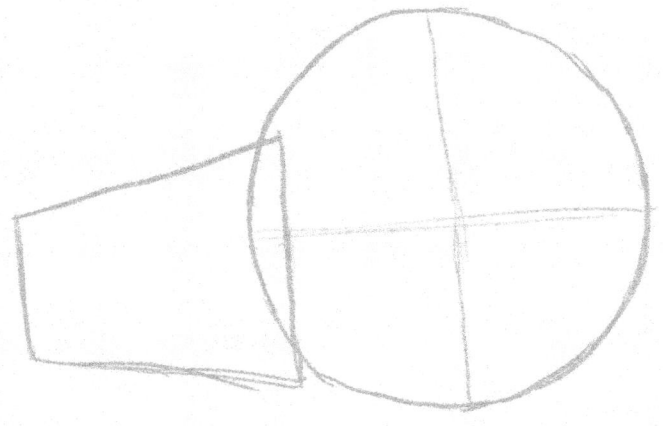

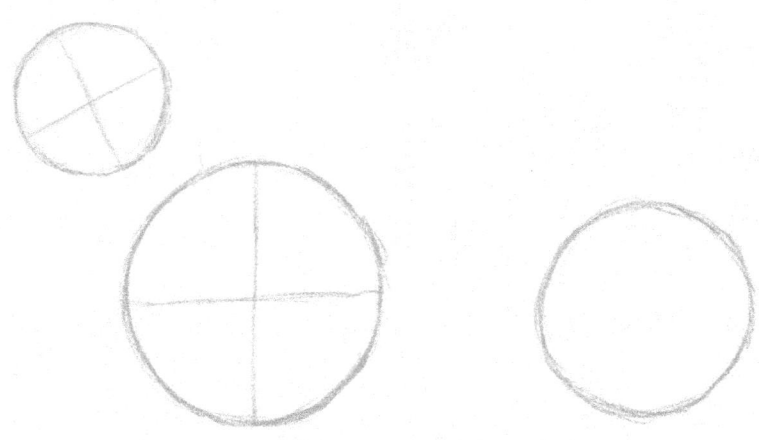

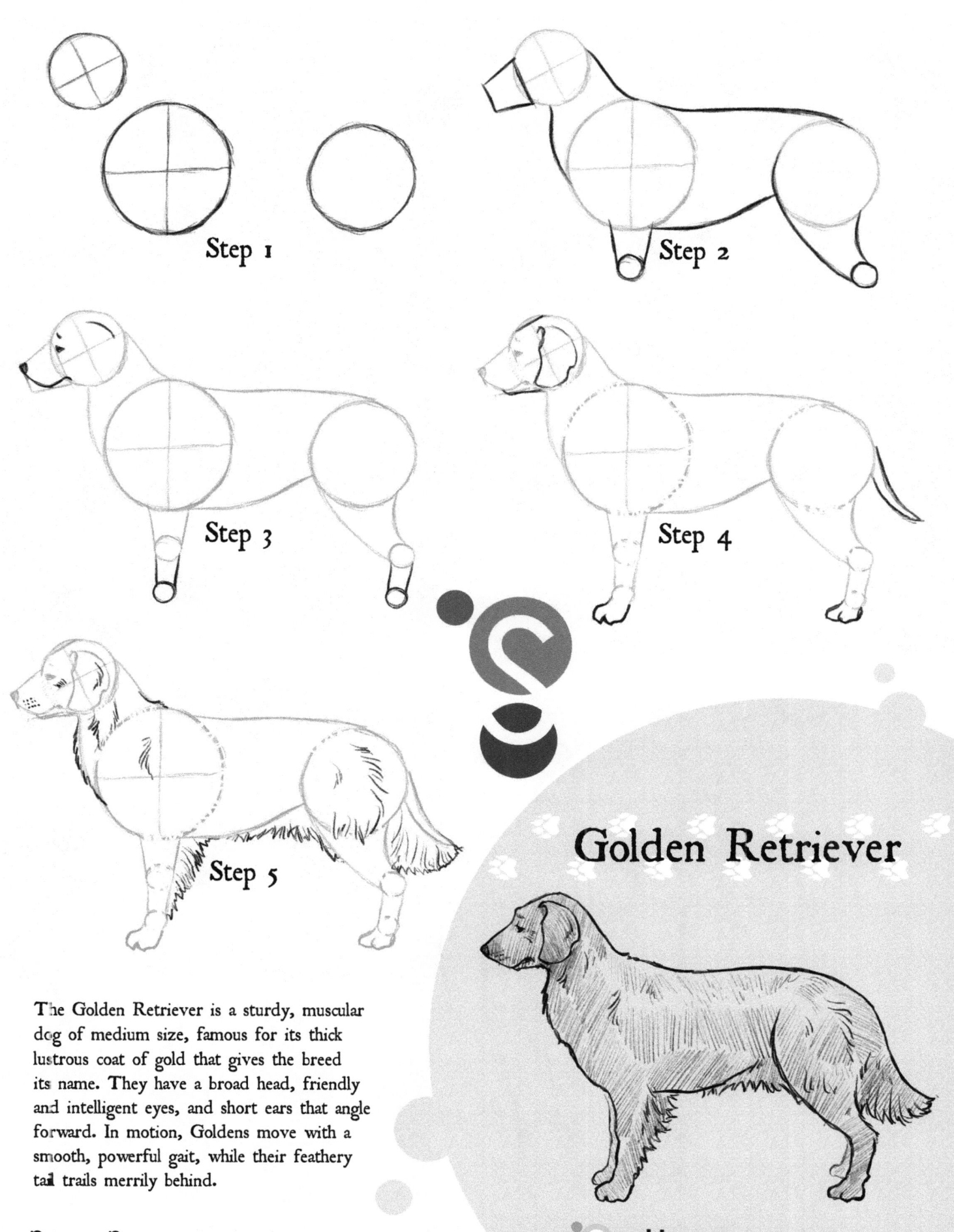

Golden Retriever

Step 1
Step 2
Step 3
Step 4
Step 5

The Golden Retriever is a sturdy, muscular dog of medium size, famous for its thick lustrous coat of gold that gives the breed its name. They have a broad head, friendly and intelligent eyes, and short ears that angle forward. In motion, Goldens move with a smooth, powerful gait, while their feathery tail trails merrily behind.

Drawing Dogs
Tutorials and Sketchbook

THE SELTZER METHOD

Drawing Dogs Tutorials and Sketchbook

THE Seltzer METHOD

Drawing Dogs
Tutorials and Sketchbook

THE Seltzer METHOD

Greyhound

The Greyhound is an ancient breed with an unknown origin. In the middle ages, nobles used their speed and endurance to chase deer and hares, in the hopes of turning them towards the hunters in the confusion.

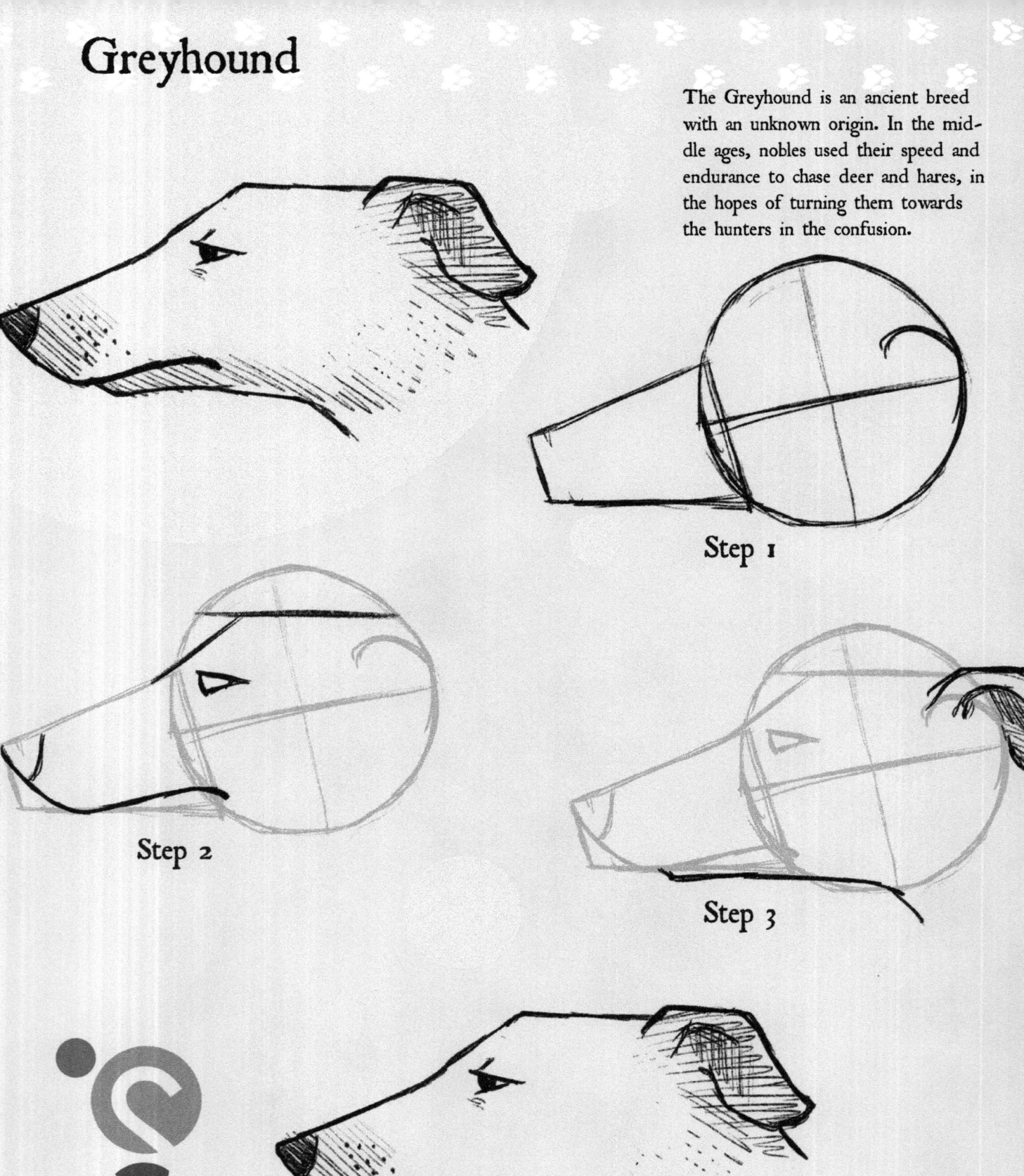

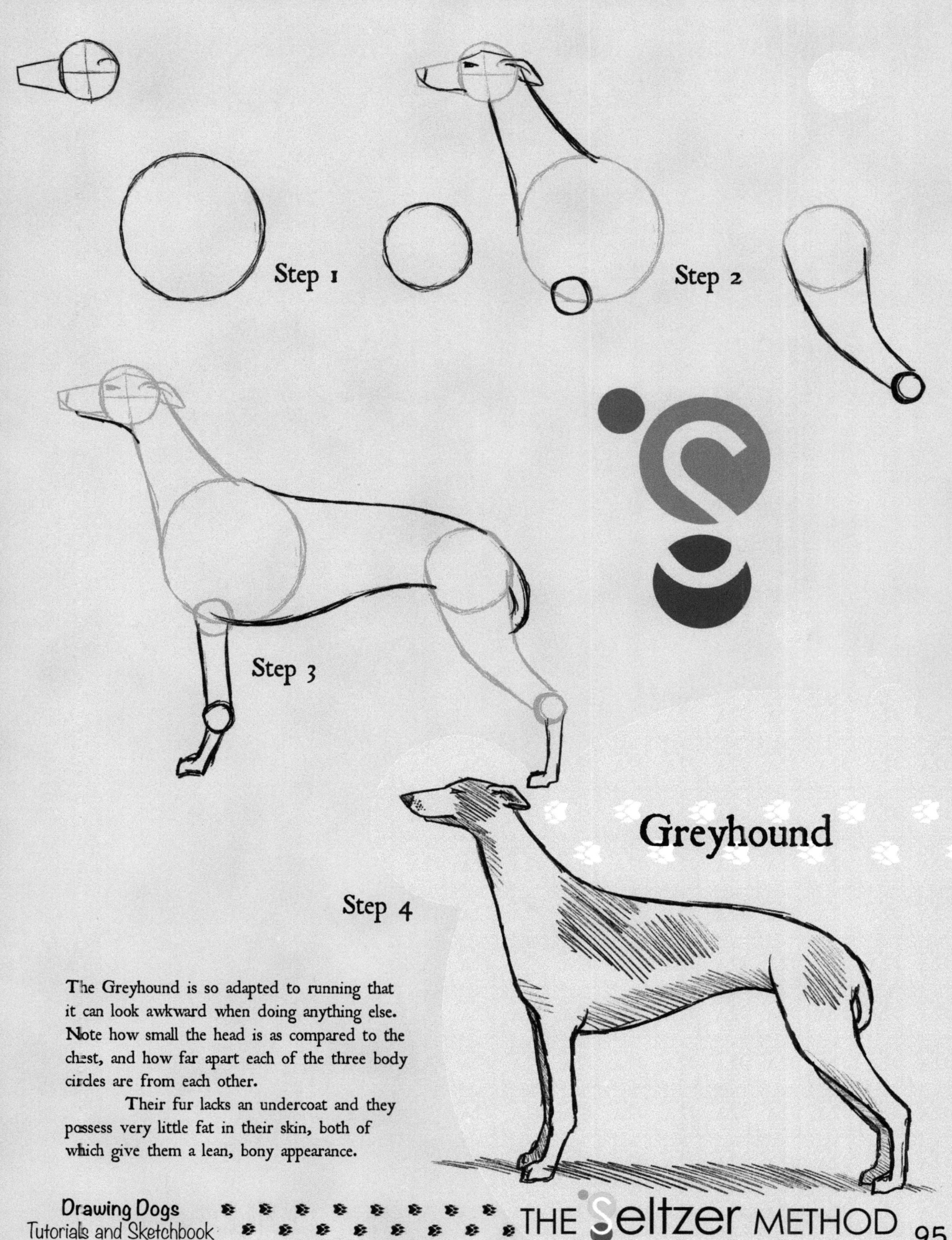

Greyhound

Step 1

Step 2

Step 3

Step 4

The Greyhound is so adapted to running that it can look awkward when doing anything else. Note how small the head is as compared to the chest, and how far apart each of the three body circles are from each other.

Their fur lacks an undercoat and they possess very little fat in their skin, both of which give them a lean, bony appearance.

Drawing Dogs
Tutorials and Sketchbook

THE SELTZER METHOD

Drawing Dogs
Tutorials and Sketchbook

THE Seltzer METHOD

99

Poodle

Poodles originated in Northern Europe sometime in the Middle Ages as a hunting dog. They are extremely smart and well rounded; able to run fast, jump high, sniff out prey, fetch, and obey commands.

Step 1

Step 2

Step 3

Step 4

Poodles have hair much like a person and not like the fur of other mammals. This means that their hair can be styled in many different ways, the most common of which is the poodle cut which we just drew. But if left unstyled, the poodle will become shaggy and look more like a sheep dog.

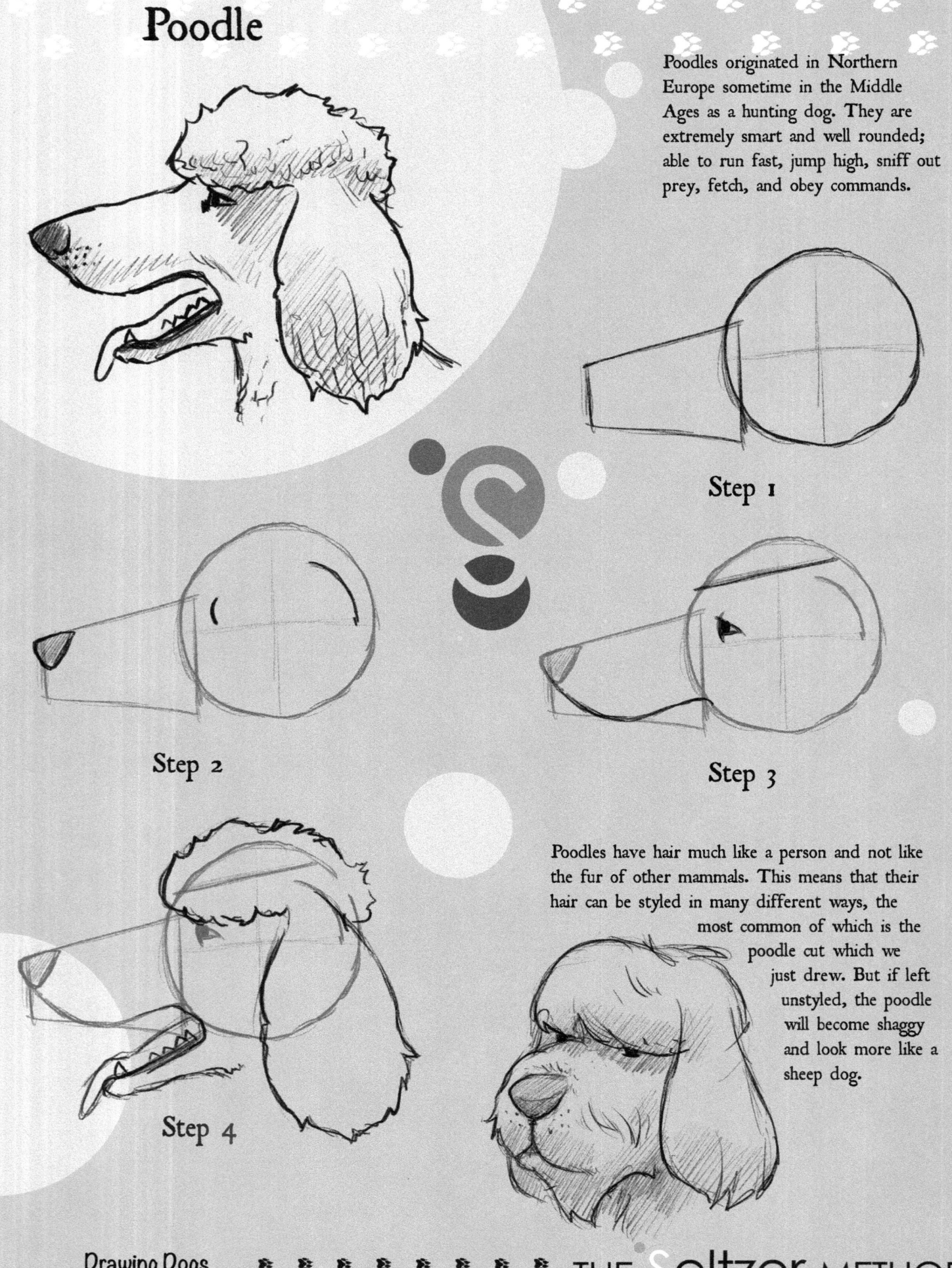

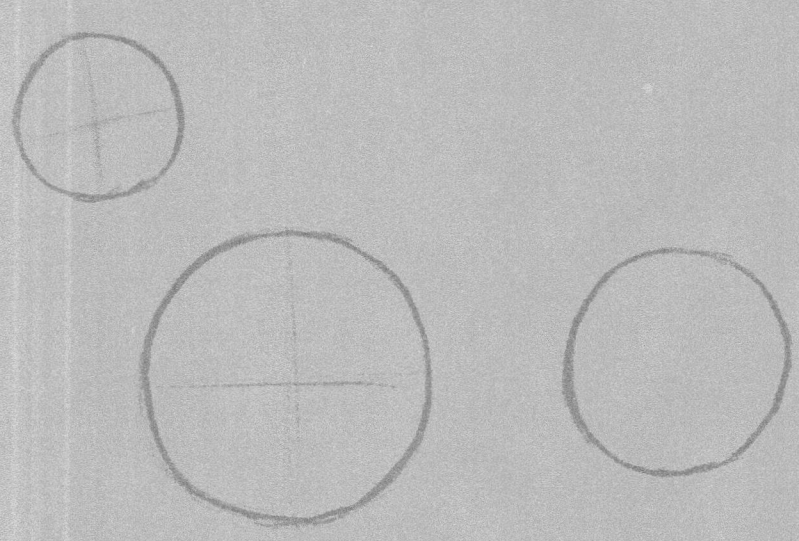

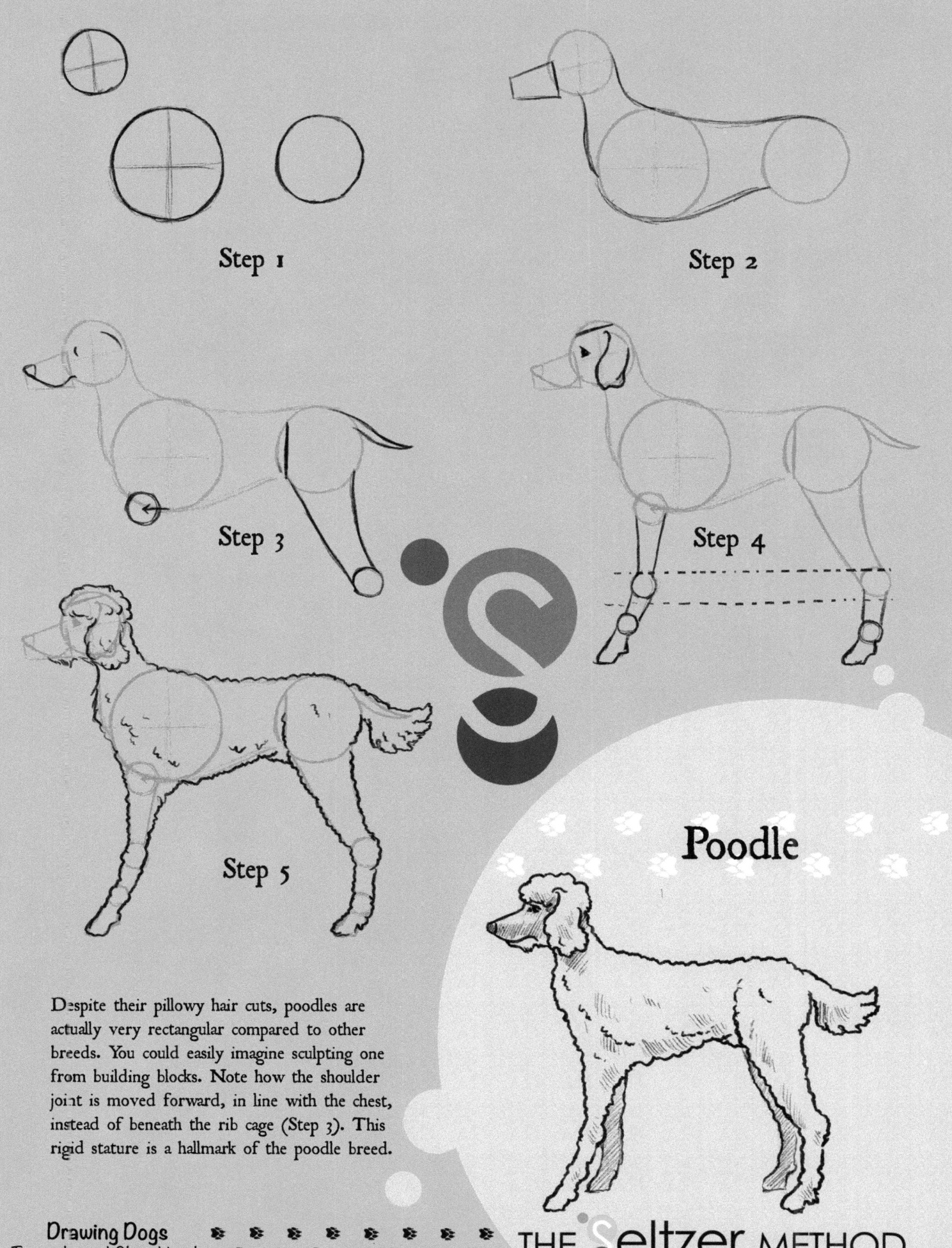

Saint Bernard

The St. Bernard dog has an unusual backstory. It was bred specifically to rescue travelers who became stranded in the snowy passes of the Alps. These strong dogs helped the monks of Great Saint Bernard Hospice to locate travelers and transport them to safety.

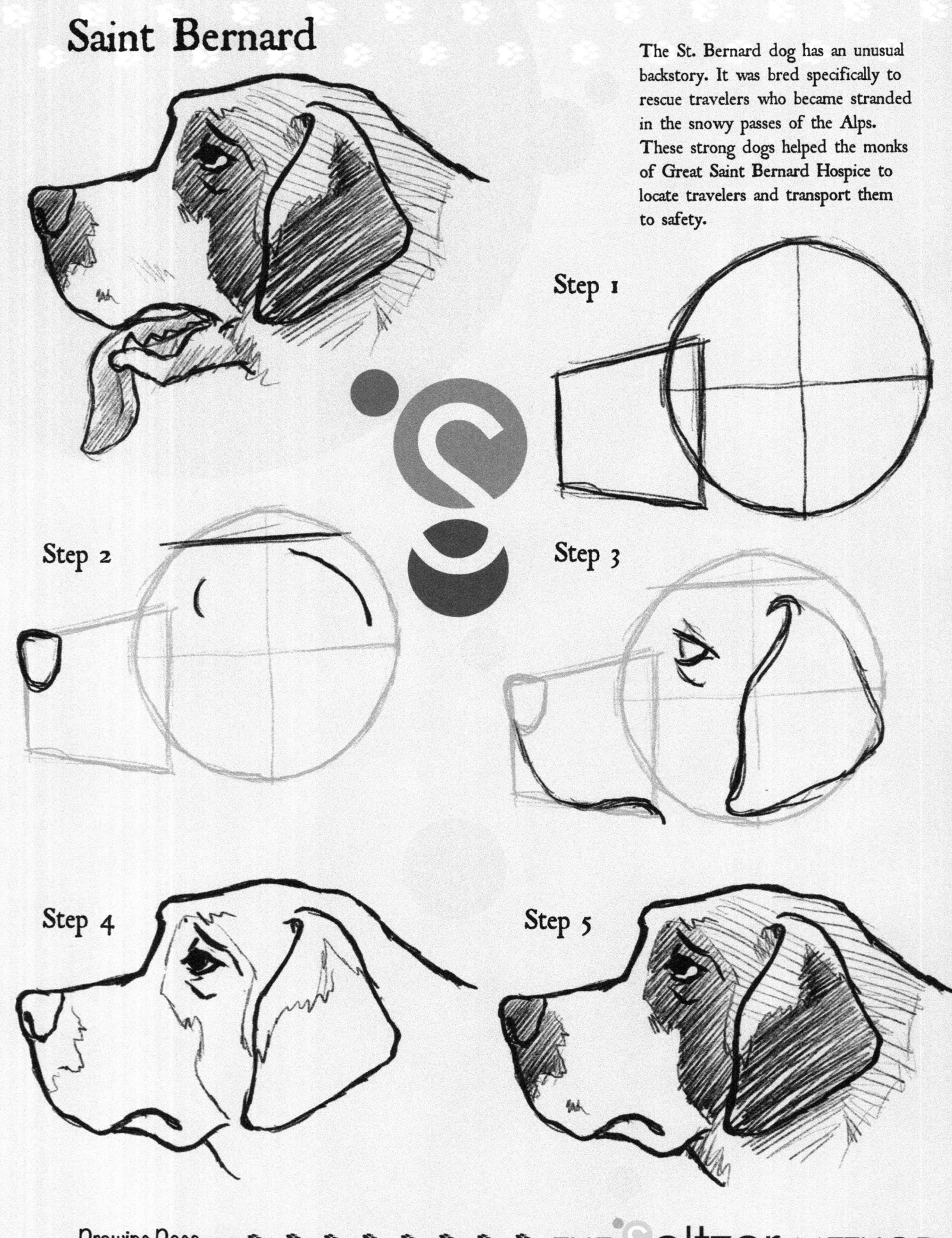

Step 1

Step 2

Step 3

Step 4

Step 5

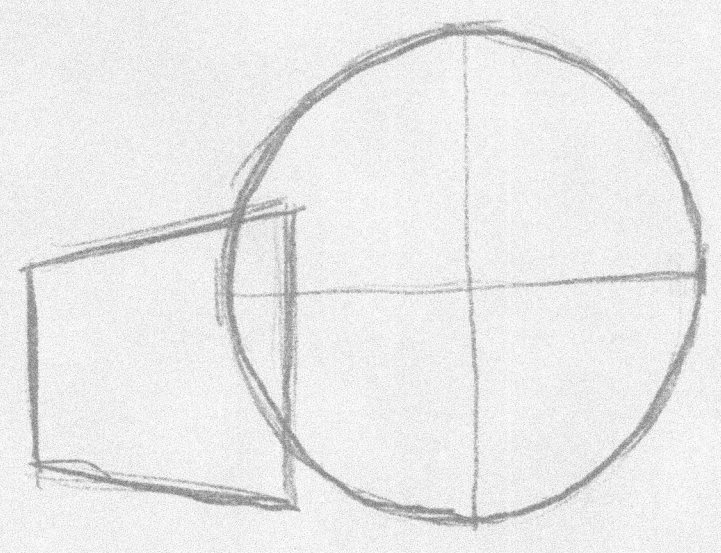

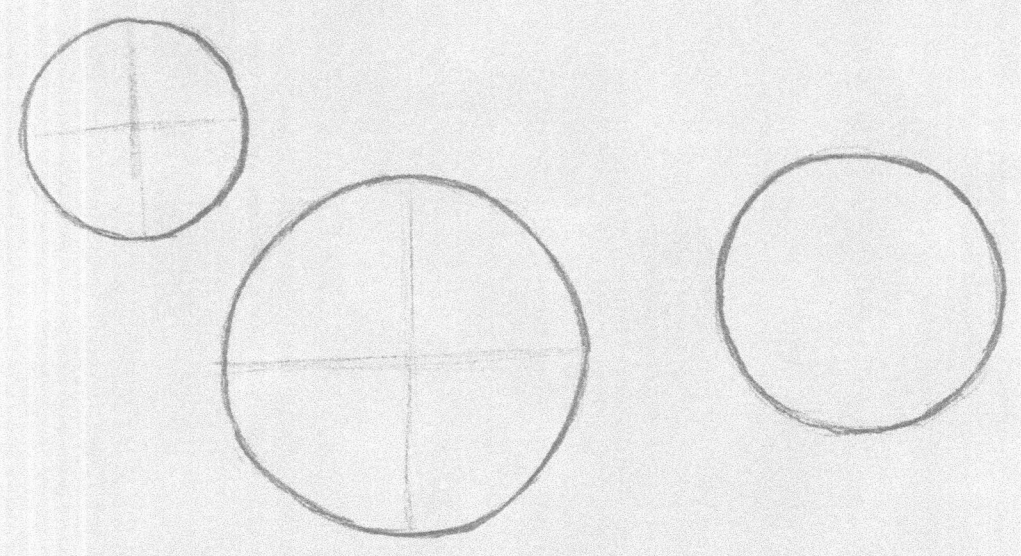

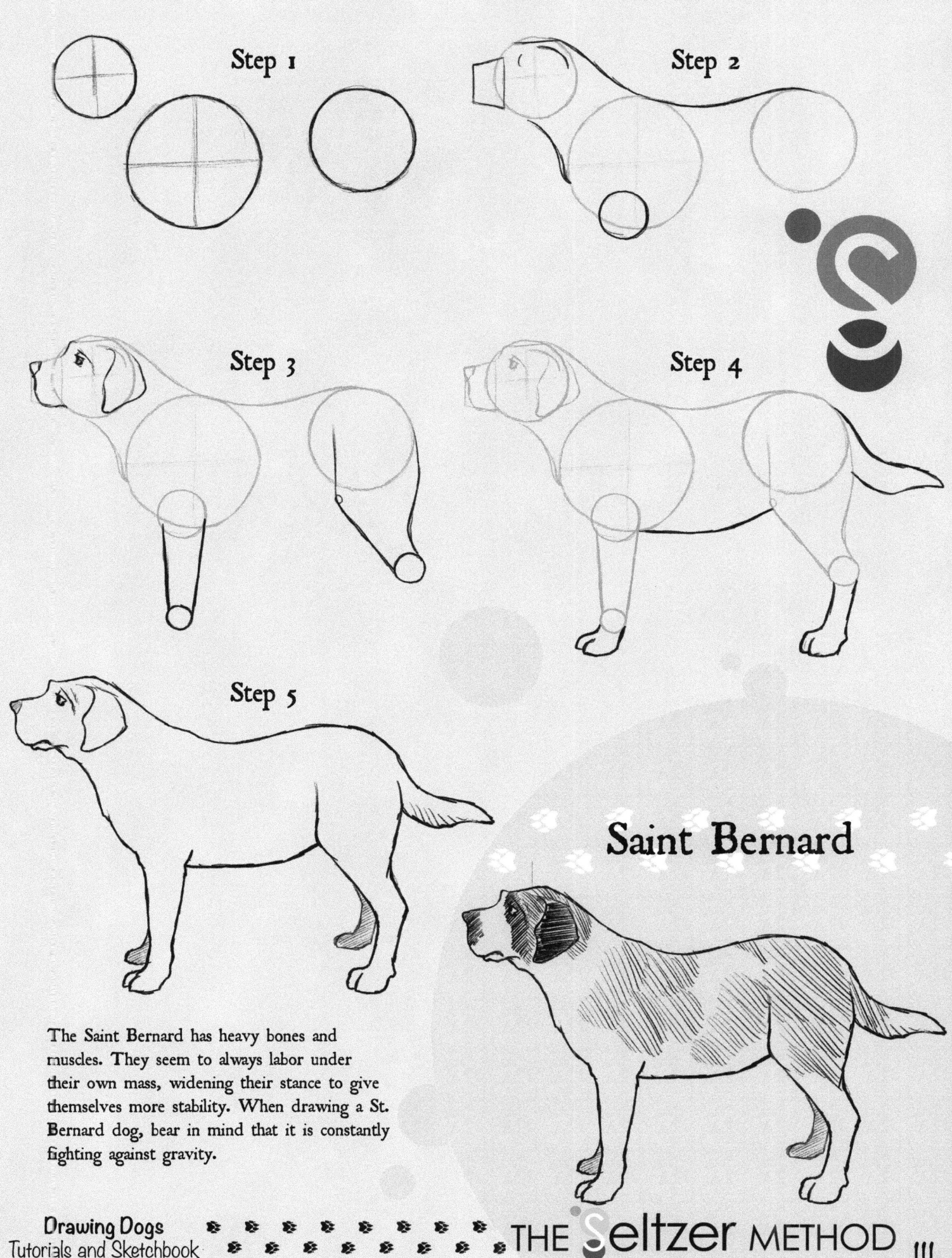

Saint Bernard

Step 1
Step 2
Step 3
Step 4
Step 5

The Saint Bernard has heavy bones and muscles. They seem to always labor under their own mass, widening their stance to give themselves more stability. When drawing a St. Bernard dog, bear in mind that it is constantly fighting against gravity.

Drawing Dogs
Tutorials and Sketchbook

THE Seltzer METHOD

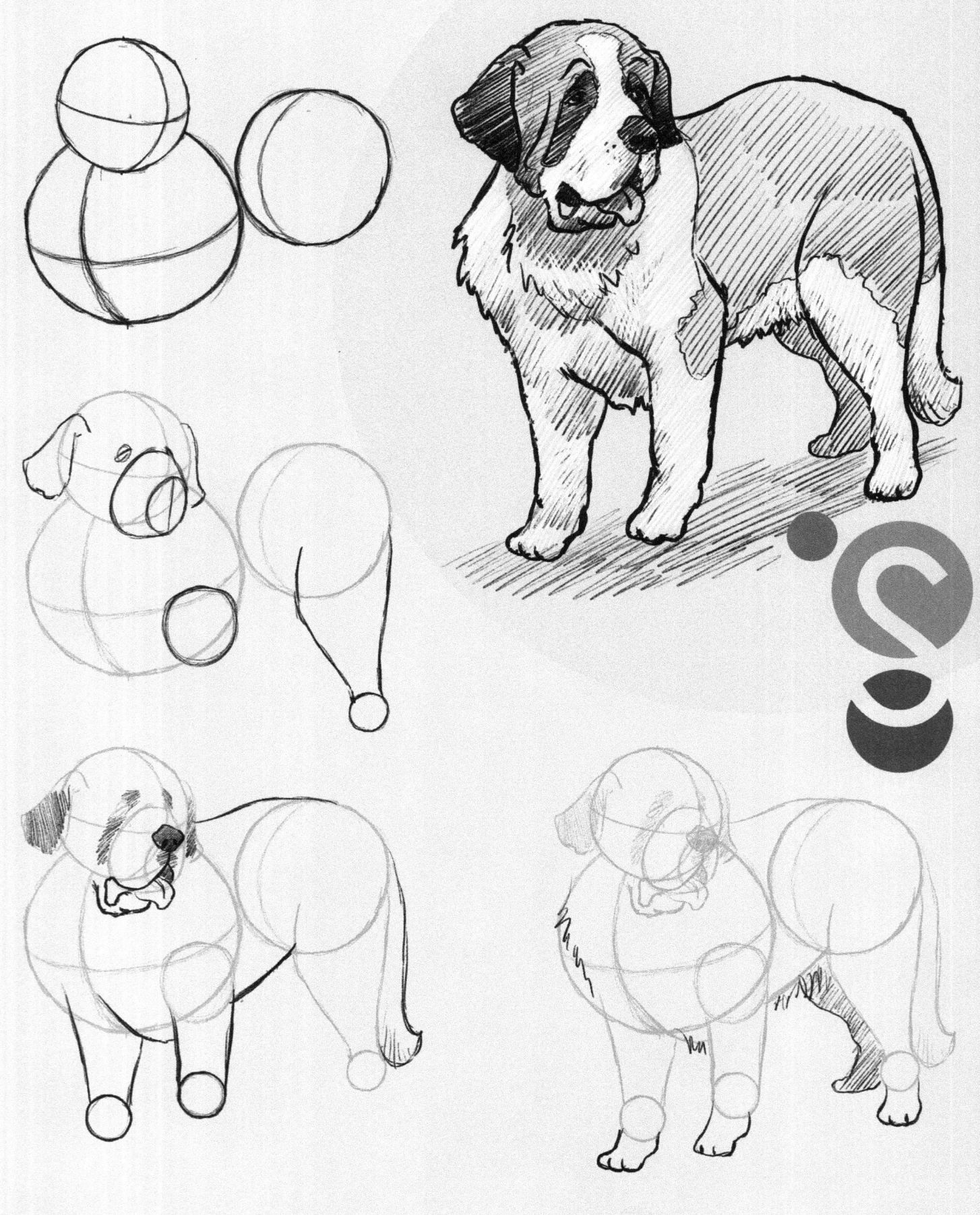

Drawing Dogs
Tutorials and Sketchbook

THE SELTZER METHOD

Drawing Dogs
Tutorials and Sketchbook

THE SELTZER METHOD

115

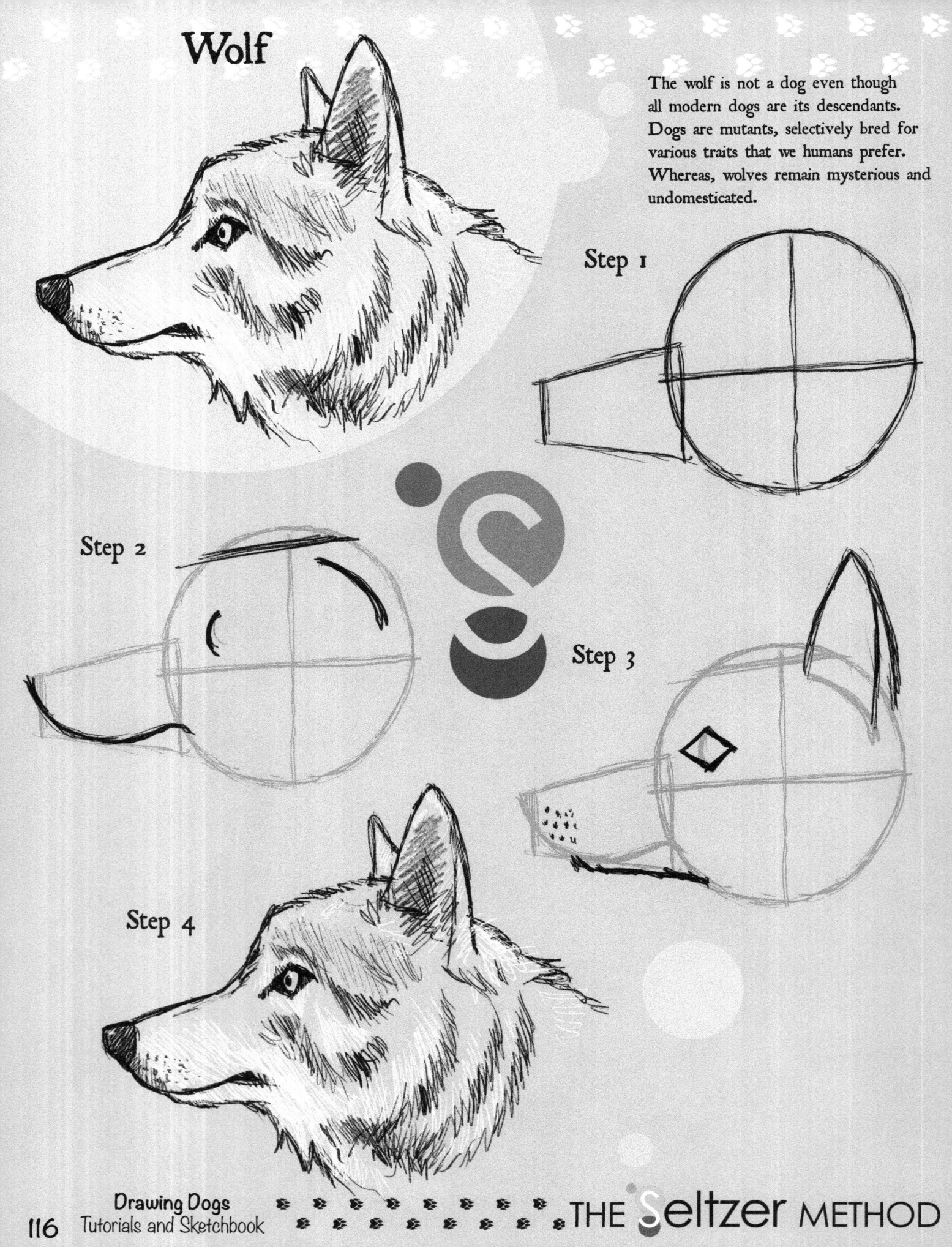

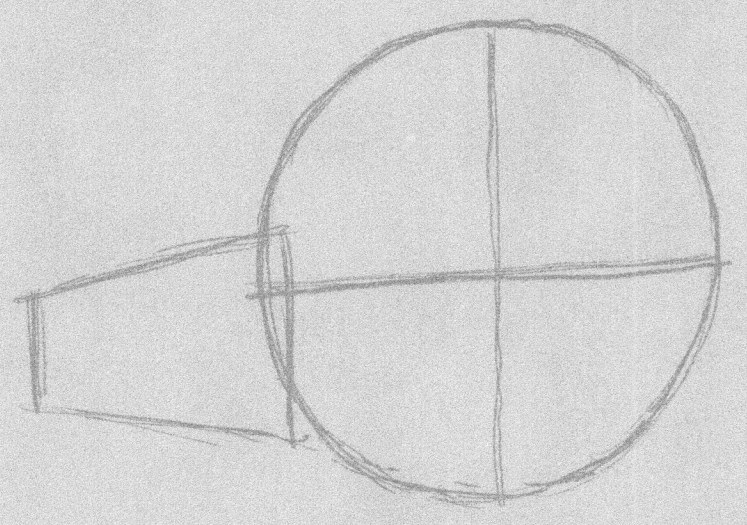

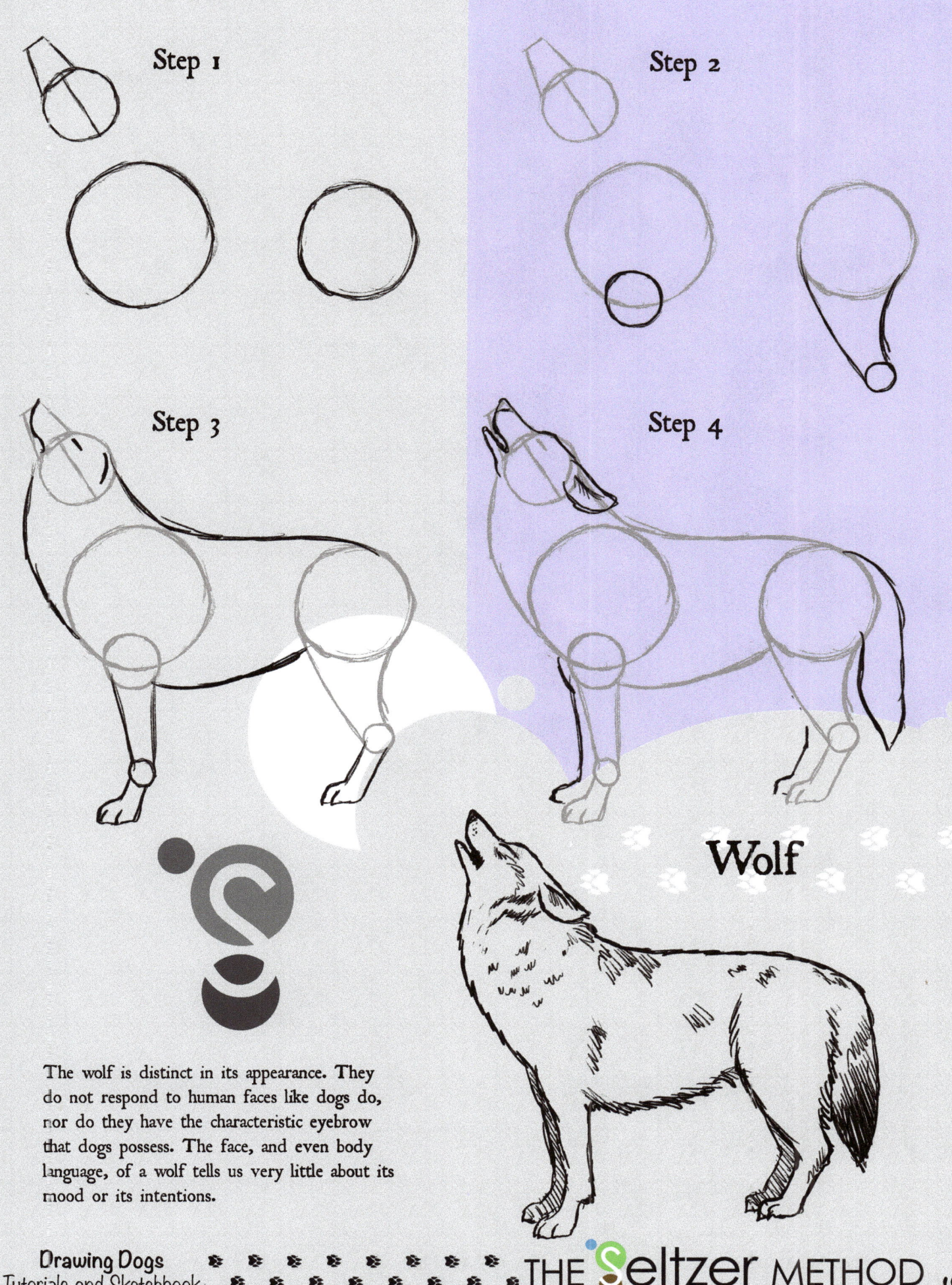

Step 1
Step 2
Step 3
Step 4

Wolf

The wolf is distinct in its appearance. They do not respond to human faces like dogs do, nor do they have the characteristic eyebrow that dogs possess. The face, and even body language, of a wolf tells us very little about its mood or its intentions.

Drawing Dogs
120 Tutorials and Sketchbook

THE seltzer METHOD

Drawing Dogs Tutorials and Sketchbook — THE Seltzer METHOD — 123